ALCHEMY OF LIGHT

Working with the
Primal Energies
of Life

ALCHEMY
of
LIGHT

*Working with the
Primal Energies
of Life*

LLEWELLYN VAUGHAN-LEE

First published in the United States in 2007 by
The Golden Sufi Center
P.O. Box 456, Point Reyes Station, California 94956.
www.goldensufi.org

Second printing 2013.

Printed and bound by Thomson-Shore, Inc.
Cover design by Anat Vaughan-Lee.

Library of Congress Cataloging-in-Publication Data

Vaughan-Lee, Llewellyn.
    Alchemy of light : working with the primal energies of life /
    by Llewellyn Vaughan-Lee.
        p. cm.
    Includes bibliographical references and index.
    ISBN 978-1-890350-13-0 (pbk. : alk. paper)
    1. Spiritual life. 2. Light--Religious aspects. I. Title.
    BL624.V3775 2007
    297.4'4--dc22
                                2007011881

CONTENTS

PREFACE

Throughout this book, in an effort to maintain continuity and simplicity of text, God, the Great Beloved, is referred to as He. Of course, the Absolute Truth is neither masculine nor feminine. As much as It has a divine masculine side, so It has an awe-inspiring feminine aspect.

There isn't
a particle in creation
that doesn't carry
Your Light
yesterday I was asking others
for a sign of You
today there isn't a sign
that isn't of
You

Jâmî

Light,
my light,
the world-filling light,
the eye-kissing light, heart-sweetening light!

Ah, the light dances, my darling,
at the centre of my life;
the light strikes, my darling, the chords of my love;
the sky opens, the wind runs wild,
laughter passes over the earth.

The butterflies spread their sails on the sea of light.
Lilies and jasmines surge up
on the crest of the waves
of light.

The light is shattered into gold on every cloud,
my darling, and it scatters gems in profusion.

Mirth spreads from leaf to leaf, my darling,
and gladness without measure.
The heaven's river has drowned its banks
and the flood of joy is abroad.

Tagore

1.
WORKING WITH LIGHT

For with thee is the fountain of life:
in thy light shall we see light.

Psalms 36:9

When God created the intellect, He asked it
"Who am I?" but the intellect was silent.
So God daubed his eyes with the kohl of the light of
divine oneness. Then the intellect said
"You are God!"

Abû 'l-Husayn an-Nûrî[1]

AWAKENING TO OUR OWN LIGHT

Our Higher Self carries a light that belongs to God. When we are born, we carry a spark of this light into our human incarnation; it illuminates the experiences of our early childhood, showing us a world that is fully alive, full of magic and wonder. But slowly, as the adult world closes around us, the spark of our Higher Self gets covered over by the dust and debris of the world, of our conditioning, our desires, our concern with success and failure, our need to compete; it "fades into the common light of day."[2] It might reappear briefly, as the light of conscience that tries to point us in the right direction or the spark of intuition that comes unbidden into our consciousness. But mostly it is hidden, forgotten like the wonder of the world we saw as children. We no longer see the world by the bright light of what is real; we see "through a glass darkly," through the shadowy, distorting light of the ego.

But the moment can come when, through the grace of God, the spark within us rekindles and we see again with its light. This is the most precious moment in the life of a soul, when we reconnect with our divine nature, when the journey Home begins.

Our reawakening to this light can take many forms: we might meet a teacher, be inspired by a spiritual text, or in a sudden unexplained moment of truth experience our eternal nature. Whatever the outer form, inwardly the moment is the same: the Higher Self gives us an energy that comes into our heart and the spark of light that is our gift from God begins to glow. The light of the Self awakens and brings its divine consciousness into our life. In this light we glimpse our true nature and the divine in life all around us. Usually the glimpse lasts just for a brief moment, and then the shadows of our ego, our mind, and the world close around us again. But it is enough to turn us away from life's illusions, to draw us on the eternal search. This is the first step on the journey Home, the journey that can lead us to a full awakening to our divine nature, "the face we had before we were born."

The journey may seem serpentine, with many wrong turns and dead-ends, but this is part of the mysterious way the Self guides us. As Carl Jung says, "The right way to wholeness is made up of fateful detours and wrong turnings." Though we rarely realize it, through this process we are working on our light, helping it to shine more brightly. This is the light that guides us on our way, that shows us the path we need to follow; without it we are lost, the journey is just a succession of illusions. When it becomes obscured through our ego or negative patterns, we stumble or lose our way; but then, through longing or despair, through the cries of our heart or the diligence of our practices, or simply through grace, we look to it again, and the light returns to guide us on, glowing brighter each time as our recognition of our need for it deepens.

As the journey takes us on our way, the light within us attracts us to the spiritual practices and the path that can help in its evolution. We might be drawn to music, because the nature of our light responds to music. Or we are drawn to a path of service, because our light can express itself most fully through helping others. Or we find that we are attracted to spiritual practices, to meditation, awareness of the breath, chanting, or to "inner work," because this is the way our light can free itself most easily from the dust that covers it. Many meditation disciplines and other spiritual practices are specifically designed to help reveal and brighten the light within us, to help us bring its higher consciousness into our life. And the processes of inner work, the psychological and spiritual work of purification and inner transformation, clear an inner space, uncluttered by negative psychological patterns or resistances, where we can have more access to our own light.

Through the wisdom and practical guidance of a path, we learn to see ourself and the world around us with this light. We learn to live a life that nourishes the soul rather than just the ego, that is truly creative and reflects our real nature. We also learn how to work with this light. Through the practice of spiritual discrimination, for example, we learn to distinguish between the light of the Self and the deceptive light of the ego; we see how the ego, frightened of losing its power and control, tries to obscure our real light and misguide us. We discover how subtly and easily we are betrayed by ourself and learn how to regain our true center when we have been misled. We recognize the attraction of the darkness of our lower nature; sometimes we have to choose between our darkness and our light, or fight against negative forces within us, confront and transform our anger and fears. We are taught the wisdom of humility and of learning from our mistakes, and we learn to avoid getting caught by arrogance or false humility that can keep us in the ego's shadowlands where our lower nature can so easily grip us.

Slowly the path and its practices free us from our negative tendencies and give us access to more and more of our light, more of its consciousness. And as we diligently work upon ourself through our devotions and inner work—as we "polish the mirror of our heart"—so the light within us grows. And this light works its mysterious chemistry, opening life in unexpected ways, revealing more of its magic and wonder. Also, as our light grows, we attract a higher light, a light from the inner world of pure spirit. This is the mystery of "light upon light" in which "light rises towards light and light comes down upon light."

The light within us and the light from above then work together, growing in strength and purity, helping us on our journey. In fact the journey *is* the light transforming us, revealing itself within and around us. What we think is our evolution is the evolution of the light of our true nature, expressing itself in our inner and outer life and expanding our consciousness. There is a great difference between a consciousness that sees with the reflected light of the ego and one that sees with the true light of the Self. The ego exists in a world of distortions and patterns of control that are antithetical to the Self. The light of the Self burns away these distortions, though this is often a painful process—to become free of the many chains that bind us, we have to lose what we have believed most precious.

All through this process the light within us grows and becomes more and more a part of our life. Usually this happens so gradually that we hardly notice it, though sometimes we go through times of transition when we are

painfully or gladly made aware of our expanded consciousness, as when we have to leave behind a pattern that has
protected us or a possession we have been attached to, or
when we joyfully awake to a new revelation of our true
nature and find life present in unexpected ways.

And so the journey continues, the eternal journey
from darkness to light.[3] This journey of the soul takes us
Home, where it finally reveals that the light within us *is*
the One Light. There is only one light—the light of the
heavens and the earth is the light within our own heart.
We are the light of God in the world. The light within
our heart is His light. This simple truth of the *unio mystica*
finally takes the wayfarer from the prison of the ego into
the ever-expanding dimension of our divine nature and its
true purpose; and into a direct experience of the oneness
of life.

IN SERVICE TO LIFE

Traditionally, after the state of union comes the station of
servanthood; *unio mystica*, the awareness of divine oneness, is followed by a deeper commitment to service, a
deeper involvement in life. No longer bound by the ego,
we are able to give ourself more completely in service to
the divine. We are able to realize the deep joy and privilege
of being in service to what is real. Then the real cooperative
work begins as we work with the light of divine oneness
in the world.

In the past, this work has been reserved for those
who have made the whole journey, who have traveled the
path from separation to union. But there are times in the
destiny of the world when the doors of servanthood open
wide and anyone who has access to her divine light, who

has been awakened—if just for an instant—to her true nature, is called to help with the work of the whole. We have reached such a time now, a moment in our collective evolution when the light of spiritual consciousness is needed to heal and transform the world, and all who have access to their light—at whatever stage of the journey—are needed in this work.

At this time, the relationship of light upon light has evolved in a new way. The need of the divine that calls to us within our hearts is now calling our attention to the light of the world. The world is dying through the abuses of materialism, power, and greed. But now a new light is awakening at the heart of the world, at the core of creation, which contains the potential for a whole new revelation of the divine and a new way of living in relation to the whole of life. We are needed now—not just to cultivate the divine light within ourselves—but to use our light to reawaken life to its real nature and purpose. Our light is the catalyst for the future. The consciousness of oneness that belongs to the Self is needed to awaken the world to the living oneness that is its real nature, so that it can once again fulfill its divine purpose.

The first step in our journey is to take responsibility for our own light and to learn to recognize it, to value and work with it so that it grows within us. But the next step of spiritual responsibility is to realize that it is not "our light" and that it does not belong to us. It is the light of the divine within us and belongs to the whole of life. And at this time we need to offer it back to life, to bring the light of our higher consciousness into dialogue with the awakening light within life, to help the world take the next step in its evolution.

Life is struggling to realize its oneness. Ecologically, the planet is desperate for humanity to recognize life's interdependent unity, the organic patterns that only as a whole support life. We are stepping into the arena of global consciousness and yet we have not taken real responsibility for what that means—we are still seeking our selfish goals, which the planet can no longer support. And because our materialistic culture has forgotten the sacred nature of life, we have no collective awareness that this shift into global awareness needs a spiritual foundation. We cannot build a global civilization on the sands of scientific or material progress. Unless it has a foundation in what is real, nothing can evolve—the old patterns will just re-create themselves. Do we want a world covered with the strip malls of our outer world and inner desires? Or do we want to lay the foundations for a civilization that honors the sacred unity of all of creation, the oneness inherent within life and within our souls?

This may seem an idealistic choice, naively simple in the face of the complexities of our world, its myriad, seemingly intractable problems. But once we fully recognize the dangers of our present global predicament, we also realize that only if we return to the source of life can there be any future: the band-aids offered by a surface response are no longer viable. And the return to the source is a turning from complexity to simplicity: to the simple nature of life as essence, and to the power, the healing, and the transformative potential that belong to this essence. What we know in our own journey—that a time of real crisis presents us with the opportunity to return to our own center, where we often find a transformative energy and solution beyond our surface imaginings—is also true for the world. The global crisis we now face is an opportunity to return the world to the essence of life at its source. Once that essence is scattered into the "ten thousand things," it becomes fragmented and distorted and loses its primal power; it is only in the simple essence of life that we will find the wholeness and power the world needs in order to move beyond its current predicament.

If we return to the essence of life that is within each of us, we will discover that something new is being born. What is coming into existence is not a reiteration of past patterns, but a new paradigm, a new expression of the divine—life in its divine nature recreating itself once again. And we are a necessary part of this recreation; we are needed to participate in helping the world to be reborn. Without our conscious participation the recreation of the world will not realize its potential: the light of the world will not evolve.

Taking spiritual responsibility means recognizing that we each have a part to play in this rebirth: that life needs our light in order to evolve. Without the contribution of our light life will continue to stagnate, and the realization of its oneness will not fully incarnate; it will not become a part of our collective consciousness. Humanity will not take the vital step of realizing its role as guardian of the planet. An opportunity will once again have been lost.

But if we embrace this moment and accept our responsibility, then we can be part of what is being reborn and help in the wonder of recreation. We can help humanity and the world take a great step in their evolution and lay the foundations for a civilization that honors the oneness within all of life and all of humanity. And we can fully participate in how this civilization comes into being.

WAYS OF WORKING WITH LIGHT

The way to work with our light in service to the whole begins with the simple recognition that our light is a part of the light of the world, part of the spiritual light of life.

This simple affirmation frees our light from the grip of any self-centered patterns and returns it to the oneness of life. The Sufis say, "It is the consent that draws down the grace," and this consent—for our spiritual light to be used in service to the whole—opens the door to an understanding of how to be in service. In essence this understanding comes from a dialogue of light to light: the divine light of life speaks to our light and communicates to it the ways in which it needs our light to participate in the unfolding of the whole.

This may seem like an esoteric notion, outside the scope of ordinary life, but once we recognize that our light is a part of life, part of its organic nature, we realize how natural this process is. Our light is like an individual cell of the light of life, and the consciousness within life's organic wholeness will naturally communicate with each single cell, just as the consciousness within our body communicates with each of our physical cells. Our conditioning that we are separate from the whole of life, and that spirit and matter are separate, has denied us this natural communion with the whole. Once we are free of these misperceptions and affirm that we are a part of life, we can become open to a direct communication with life.

Learning to be receptive, to listen to the guidance that comes from within, is a basic spiritual practice. Taking this practice into the arena of service to the whole will mean learning to listen for the particular way life is asking us to participate. This request can come from the outer or inner world, but it will speak to us with the simplicity of life's essence, and it will be in tune with our own essential nature. We do not need to be other than who we are; we just need to be prepared to be fully alive and awake to the need of the moment—not to be caught in our expectations or images of spiritual service. Because each individual's light is unique, the way it can participate will also be unique. Life will speak to us in our own way, guiding us to the work that needs to be done.

There are many different arenas of spiritual work at this time in which our particular light can be of service. For example we could be attracted to the fields of healing or ecology—be connected to the energy body of the planet and given the tools we need to help to free it from inner and outer energies that are polluting it. Or one could be drawn into the world of business, and be taught to work with the energies of money and commerce, to free them from the darkness that binds them with greed. Some people are being asked to work inwardly in the archetypal or imaginal world. The participation of human consciousness is needed now to help give birth to the symbols of the next age, to create the symbolic foundation of life for the next era—this is shamanic work for the whole of life, in which our light can work directly with the soul of the world. Our light could also be directed into the spiritual body of the world where it can help to awaken centers of power that are needed for the earth's evolution. In all areas of this work, life will draw our attention to where it is needed, and our light, individually or as a group, will be taught how to work with the world as a living whole.

Certain kinds of work now specifically require the light of women. There is, for example, a work of bringing into this plane of existence a particular quality or vibration of spiritual energy that is needed for the transformation of life. This is a spiritual energy that belongs to the sacredness of matter, and because women have an instinctual understanding of the sacred nature of matter, this work of transmission can only be done by women. Women carry the sacred substance of life in their spiritual centers and understand how to give this quality of light to life; in their ability to give birth, women have the natural capacity to bring the light of a soul into the physical world of matter and thus awaken the spiritual potential of matter. Women also understand the connections between people and the connections within life; at this time women are needed to bring a seed of pure light into life where it can create new forms and new patterns of interrelationship that are essential to the healing and transformation of life.

Many new kinds of connections and relationships need to be made in order to support the manifestation of life's inherent oneness, connections that will link together diverse people, groups, ideas, and many other elements now separate, into new patterns of relationship. This is also work that requires our light: the divine light within us can create connections and patterns of relationship that our rational consciousness with its linear framework cannot. Our light moves more quickly and can bypass many of the resistances that could obstruct the changes that are needed. Fully alive in the moment, not caught in patterns of the past, our light can respond to all the currents flowing into each moment—both visible and hidden—and can bring about unexpected and seemingly miraculous results and happenings.

The connections need to be made on all levels. We are moving away from the past era's focus on individuality to an understanding of the interconnectedness of life in which we no longer see life as a collection of separate individuals but as a living, intricately connected web in which each part affects every other part, and the new patterns of relationship need to reflect that. This work will be done as the lights of individuals come together into groups, which then connect with other groups to form a living network of light that can support the next stage of our evolution. This must be done in a way that respects the individuality and uniqueness of each individual; otherwise we cannot contribute our unique light, play our unique note. But as these individuals and groups link together, they form a single organic body of light that can help to give birth to and contain the spiritual awakening of the world.

WE ARE THE PLACE WHERE
THE FUTURE IS BEING BORN

These are just a few of the areas of spiritual service, ways our light can participate. Each of us will find the unique way that our light can be used. In giving our light back to life, we will discover the beauty and wonder of our inherent connection to the greater whole, not just on the physical level but within the spiritual dimension of ourselves, the dimension of the Self. Spiritual texts tell us that when we realize our individual Self, our true nature, we also realize the universal Self: the individual *atman is* the universal *atman*. At a certain stage on our journey we can leave behind, if only for a moment, our individual self and step into this greater dimension of awareness. This awareness usually comes only after many years of spiritual practice. But due to the need of the time, we are being given the opportunity to live it *now*, regardless of how far we have come on our journey. By stepping fully into the arena of global spiritual service, we step into the greater dimension of the whole.

As our light meets and interacts with the light of the whole, something unexpected happens: our light becomes a catalyst, awakening life to new possibilities, giving the organic wholeness of life new ways to evolve. The forms that will develop out of these awakened possibilities will evolve more gradually, as the structures of our civilization change. But this interaction of light with light gives life the spiritual energy and consciousness that the world needs to make this shift into the future. In this meeting of lights, life's oneness comes alive in a new way, including us and yet also taking us beyond our sense of what it means to be alive. To be part of the formation of a new era, a new way of being with life and with the divine, is to be invited to the dance of creation, the orgasmic rebirth of the sacred. We have been so conditioned to believe that we are separate from life and that the planet is something other than us that we cannot imagine what it would mean to return to the center of the circle where the Real bursts into manifestation, where this joyous eruption of cosmic energy takes place.

"Light upon light" is a real, dynamic happening in which the divine oneness of life and our own consciousness interact, drawing us into the mystery of creation and what it means to be fully alive. Life is not a battle to be fought or a struggle to survive; it may contain battles and struggles, but in essence it is the divine coming into being, expressing itself in a myriad of ways, each of which honors and celebrates the Creator. When we return to this axis of creation, we reconnect with the part of ourself that our culture has forgotten: our natural way of being with the divine in life, not just as a God we pray to in times of tribulation, but as something as ordinary and simple and necessary as the breath. The divine is *alive*. It is not a concept, not a fixed idea or an icon, but a dynamic, living presence that permeates everything that exists.

Our light is the light of God being given back to life. We are the messengers of the divine, the means by which the divine wants to reconnect itself with its creation. We carry the secrets of this recreation in our spiritual centers, and it is through our light that they will manifest, as we give our light back to the light of the whole.

The seeds for the future are in this interaction of light with light. If we will embrace our responsibility for our part in the world's recreation, we can be awake at the dawn, at the moment when the world shifts on its axis and a breath from the beyond blows away the debris of the last era. We can be the future welcoming God back into His world.

2.

THE LIGHT OF THE WORLD

O Light of light, Thy light illumines the people of
heaven and enlightens the people of earth.
O Light of all light.
Thy light is praised by all light.

Prayer attributed to Mohammad

A LIGHT TO SEE BY

We see this world around us through the light of our consciousness. Our eyes and other senses are the physical mechanism by which we perceive the world, but it is through our consciousness that we experience its colors and beauty, and the richness of the experiences life offers us. Our experience of life expands as our consciousness expands: we have more light to see by, and our experience grows fuller, richer, deeper.

When our consciousness is confined within the limited scope of our mind and ego, the world we experience is filled with the images we have created. We are conditioned to think that the world defined by these individual and collective images is the real world. This is the world we think we know, the world into which we are born and from which only death can free us, the world in which we struggle, suffer, and sometimes taste a fleeting happiness. And while spiritual texts may tell us that this world is an illusion, it appears very real to our senses and mind; it seems almost madness to assert that it is not the reality it appears to be in the light of our limited individual consciousness that is rooted in the mind and ego.

But within the heart of every human being there lies hidden another light which reveals a world beyond the one perceived by our ego-consciousness. This is the light of the Self, which is a direct knowing of God. It is this light that draws us back to God, that calls us on the search for Truth, and reveals the real nature of life. Then life and the soul speak to us and tell us about the journey of the soul, the journey back to the Source. When this light within the heart is awakened, we begin to experience a whole different world.

The shift from a world seen by just the light of the ego to a world seen by the light of the Self can be either a subtle or a dramatic awakening. We might gradually sense something else present within ourself and within the world, a quality of peace, love, light or pure being. Or we could undergo a mind-shattering expansion of consciousness, in which the ego is pushed aside by the power of the Real, or, as in a Zen experience of *satori*, we experience the world unveiled, *as it is*, unmediated by any thought or concept. For each of us this moment in which the light of the Self comes into our world is unique, but it is an awakening to our real nature and the real nature of life. The world revealed by this light is the world we have always known, and yet it is completely new.

THE LIGHT WITHIN THE WORLD

At the core of the world there is also a light that belongs to God. This light carries the secret of His intention, of His hidden purpose. Where the light within the heart is a direct knowing of God that calls us on the search for Truth, the light within the world is a knowing of the divine purpose of His manifestation, of His revelation of Himself in His world. The light within the world calls us to see this secret, to make it conscious, that we may begin to see the world by the light of His divine intention.

The light at the core of the world has always been present, but hidden, waiting to awaken, just as our own light lies hidden in our own heart until it is awakened. And just as there is a moment of grace in our individual life when the light of the Self awakens in us, there also comes a moment in cosmic time when the light of the world awakens. On our individual journey, this awakening often happens at a time of despair: our soul, desolate in a world without meaning, calls out, and our divine light responds, revealing to us our divine nature which we had forgotten, and bringing meaning, color, and life back to our world. So also does the light within the world awaken, in response to humanity's cry of despair.

The world today knows the meaning of desolation; what is sacred has been desecrated and denied. Something within the world and within the hearts of those who love the world and its Creator has called out, and the light within the world has responded. Those who recognize what is really happening to the world, who experience its suffering and sorrow, have reminded the divine of an ancient pledge not to let the spirit of the world die, not to let this desecration be so complete that nothing can be reborn. This is a real danger: there comes a moment when the cycle of self-destruction and forgetfulness begins to pollute the energies that can recreate life to such a degree that the sacred cannot be reborn. We have now reached that moment in the life cycle of our planet. Our ecological devastation and—more significantly—our collective desecration of all that is sacred are polluting the spiritual energy of life itself. Through our self-centeredness we are poisoning the spiritual lifeblood of the planet such that the situation has become almost irreversible.

When the collective forgetfulness of humanity reaches a certain point, then humanity reverts to an earlier stage in its development. We see indications of this reversion already in our collective greed for material possessions that have no spiritual purpose—that do not really nourish us. We are reverting to a tribal self-preservation and our survival instinct is brought to bear not upon any real need itself but upon our possessions, the accumulation and protection of which have become our goal. A fundamental spiritual purpose to life is being buried under this debris. Soon it will be lost to our collective consciousness, and humanity will have regressed to a less spiritually developed stage. The signs of this are all around us, especially in the West, but they are obscured by the glitter of our possessions, by the toys of our technological development. But what is the purpose of all this outer development if the music of the soul is lost, if the spiritual purpose of life is forgotten? "For what shall it profit a man, if he shall gain the whole world, and lose his own soul?"[1]

WORKING WITH THE LIGHT OF THE WHOLE

The awakening of the light of the world is an opportunity for us to reverse this cycle of forgetfulness and to remember why we are here. Through this light we can redeem the world and all of humanity, because the light of the world is the light of the whole of life, the whole planet, the whole of humanity. When the light of the world awakens in us, we can redeem what has been desecrated and empower the whole of humanity to take the next step in its evolution.

Without this light we cannot see where we are going or the work that needs to be done. Nor can we be awake to the world that is really around us, the world of His divine purpose. We remain caught in our self-destructive dream of material progress.

The souls of those who remember God have called out and the light of the world has responded. We have taken the first step. The collective may still be caught in its addiction to consumerism, but there is a growing network of individuals and groups who are working for the evolution of the whole. They have seen the abyss in front of us and recognized our responsibility for the planet. They have also glimpsed the opportunities within our present situation. Their work is to bring the light of the whole into our individual everyday life, so that it can transform life. Only the light of the world, which is the light of the whole, can transform the world, just as only the light of the Self can transform an individual. On our individual journey, we know that without this light there can be no real or lasting transformation. We have yet to fully realize how this also holds true for the whole world.

In the transformation of an individual, one of the first steps is to create a body of light that is like a womb for our spiritual rebirth. Through our practices and devotions, our prayers, meditation, and aspiration, we create this body of light with our own life energy, which is why traditionally a period of introversion, or "brooding," is needed for this stage of spiritual work—energy that normally flows outward into life is circulated inwardly. This container needs to be strong enough to withstand any negative forces from the ego or the psyche that may try to interfere with our spiritual awakening. The body of light is the container for the divine light that is given, which is the spark that creates the divine child within us.

In the same way, individuals and groups have begun to create a container for working with the divine light of the world, a container created from the light of their own aspirations and service. This container is made of the connections between them; the container *is* the network that links them together. This is not simply an inert container for what will be given—that misunderstanding of the nature of the container limits the work that can be done. The network of light is itself part of the energy of transformation.

The connections that are being made now are a necessary part of the process, but this is just a preliminary stage. The next step will be to infuse this container, this living network, with the light of the whole, and see how it responds: to see whether it can hold together, contain the higher forces of a spiritual awakening, and withstand the negative energies of the collective.

In the transformation of an individual this is often a crucial stage. Has the work of preparation—the inner work—created a container for real spiritual consciousness? If certain aspects of the inner work have not been done thoroughly, the individual can become inflated, or psychologically or psychically unbalanced, by the influx of divine energy. This moment in the transformation of an individual presents many dangers. With the light of the world there will also be dangers. An individual participating in this work might not fully acknowledge that this light is for the whole and could take the light of the world for his own. Individuals or groups might try to use the light for their own purposes, even with good intentions, not recognizing or respecting the much bigger process in which they are participating. As the vibration of this light is very specifically designed for its real purpose, it only works properly within the container of the whole, as a part of the organic wholeness of life. If it is misused, it can become spiritually destructive. This energy *is* the whole of life, recreating itself from the highest level. It cannot be beneficially used for any other purpose.

REAL COOPERATIVE WORK

But although the light of the world belongs to the whole of creation, it also has a direct relationship to the individual. This is part of the mystery of the individual as microcosm. When Christ said, "You are the light of the world,"[2] he was acknowledging this dimension within each individual human being. Our divine light is the light of the world, and our individual light relates directly to the light of the whole. This relationship of light to light belongs to the way that oneness works within the individual and within the world. The light within the individual and the light within the world are one light, a light that in calling to us also calls to itself, evokes itself, responds to itself.

On our own mystical journey we experience this mystery of light calling to light:

> Light rises toward light and light comes down upon light, *"and it is light upon light"*.... Each time a *light rises up from you, a light comes down toward you,* and each time a flame rises from you a corresponding flame comes down toward you.[3]

The light of our aspiration draws down the light of His love. Through this relationship our light is nourished and grows, until

> the substance of light ... becomes a Whole in relation to what is of the same nature in Heaven: then it is the substance of light in Heaven which

yearns for you and is attracted by your light, and it descends toward you. This is the secret of the mystical approach.[4]

When our light has grown in this way, it experiences its essential nature: that in truth it is one light coming to meet itself, just as in the esoteric mystery of "He loves them and they love Him"—lover and Beloved are one. Then the journey changes, no longer driven by effort but carried by grace.[5]

On the journey of spiritual ascent, the relationship between the light of our aspiration, the light that rises up, and the higher light that comes down, makes the journey possible. We call to our Beloved and He comes to meet us. In the drama of the world, the light of our devotion and service calls to the light within creation. First it reminds this divine light of its pledge to save the world. Then it has to welcome this light into a world covered in forgetfulness of its divine purpose, just as we have to welcome the light of our own Self into our individual world that has been shrouded for so long in our forgetfulness of our real nature. The work of the present time is to welcome His light back into the world. And this is not the transcendent light of the inner mystical journey, but the light hidden at the core of creation. It is this light that is needed to transform our world.

Because it is in essence the same light, there can be a direct communication between the light within the individual and the light of the world, a communication based upon oneness, not upon duality. We are used to communication based on duality, which often results in misunderstanding, as duality is a paradigm of separation and differences. A relationship based upon oneness is direct and dynamic: it functions within an altogether different paradigm that is based upon an understanding of the fundamental unity of all things and the natural cooperation that arises from it.

The light of the world knows that we are one, and works within this context. Through life's essential unity it has direct access to all of life's interconnections, which are an expression of that unity. The light itself is that unity: just as the light of our soul is present throughout our body and psyche, so is the light of the world present in every cell of creation, in every thought and every dream. It is present in each atom and in all the connections between the atoms. It is a living network of light that sustains all of life.

When we relate to this light within life, we relate directly to the whole of life. This is part of the power of the relationship of light to light. When our individual light relates to the world's light, which permeates everything in life, we have direct access to all of life's interconnections, and to all of the archetypal structures that form life, that are the riverbeds through which the waters of life flow. We place ourselves at the very center of life, a center that is everywhere. In the relationship of light to light, nothing is excluded, because it is a relationship that belongs to oneness, to our essential unity and the unity of life. This relationship is not an idea, but a living reality that has the potential to bring about real change.

Through this interchange we can have a true co-creative relationship with life. We ourselves can live the mystery of "one-handed basket weaving" that Rûmî celebrates in his story of a Sufi sheikh who has had one of his hands cut off. A visitor who enters his hut without knocking sees the one-handed sheikh weaving palm-leaf baskets. "It takes two hands to weave!" the visitor exclaims. But because the sheikh has no fear of dismemberment or death, he has access to a divine hand that helps him. As he explains to his astonished visitor:

> When those anxious, self-protecting
> imaginations leave, the real,
> cooperative work begins.[6]

When we step outside the self-protecting image of our separate self, we can directly participate in the work of the whole, the mystery of working together with the forces of creation and the light of the world.

We do not yet realize the profound significance of this relationship of our individual self to the whole. The two lights need each other for this urgent work that needs to be done now in the world, just as the light from above needs the light from below for the spiritual transformation of the individual. This relationship of light to light, the light of our individual consciousness to the light of the whole, is central to the mystery of the human being, who is His secret: "Man is My secret and I am his secret."[7] The light of the human being *is* the spiritual essence of God in the world. But only when we recognize this, when we acknowledge that our light belongs to God, can it awaken to its real potential, its power for transformation. This light can transform our self and our world, but only when working in cooperation with a light that is beyond our individual consciousness. On the inner journey this is the light from above; for the work in the world it is the light at the core of creation. Without this "external" light we remain caught within the limitations of our own self and nothing new can be born. Transformation is always a cooperative undertaking.

COMMUNICATING WITH
THE LIGHT OF THE WHOLE

What is the nature of this relationship of light to light, of our consciousness to the light of the world? How does this cooperation take place? For the mystic it is always a relationship of love. Love is the basis of our existence, of our relationship to life and to God. Without love no real relationship can take place and nothing can be born. Love directly connects us to the light of the world, which speaks to our heart.

At the beginning we experience this relationship as a simple awareness of the light of the world, a simple connection of light to light. But once we recognize it as the communion of love that it is, it opens into a more conscious awareness of our place within life and of how we can contribute to the whole. Each of us has a unique part to play, a unique contribution that our individual light can make, and we each need to take the step of learning how to live our light in the world and in relation to the whole.

This communication is wonderfully simple: the light of the world *is* the whole, and so it encompasses in itself the particular way that our light can participate in its unfolding; it knows what we need to do. It speaks to our light as light to light, within a relationship of oneness, where there is no danger of misunderstanding. It shows our light its place in creation. The light of each individual vibrates at a unique frequency, and it shows us how this frequency can function in relation to the whole.

But our light is not a fixed or static entity. Life is alive; it is in continual flux. Nothing is static. The unfolding of the whole is a constantly changing, dynamic process. While it may follow certain inherent laws—for example the law of least resistance, according to which life flows like water from the source—the organic nature of life depends upon change for its survival and its evolution, and we are a part of this change. In order to participate fully, our own light sometimes needs to adapt and change to reflect changes within the whole. Because the light of the whole includes our light, the knowledge of the adaptations we need to make, along with help to do it, is also a part of the communication from light to light.

When we give our light to the light of the world, we give it the light of individual consciousness; we allow individual consciousness to be included in the light of the whole, and we help it in this process of dynamic change. Individual consciousness has a vital part to play as a catalyst in the evolution of the whole. The arrival of human consciousness on our planet speeded up life's evolution, releasing it from the laws of nature, which change very slowly, over millennia. Through our human consciousness new forms, images, and ideas can come into being; through us the intelligence of the world can be more creative. Through our light the light of the whole can evolve faster and more purposefully. In the communication of our individual light and the light of the world, both lights are quickened, in both senses of the word.

Yet we have lost this direct relationship between our individual light and the light of life. The last era's focus on individualism fostered an image of consciousness as separate from the whole, a tool for imposing our dominance over others and over nature. We have almost forgotten that in older cultures people viewed consciousness much differently, in a context of the oneness and interconnectedness of the whole world of creation. This allowed them, for example, to use their consciousness to communicate with nature in a way we can now barely imagine. Robert Wolff, who was initiated by the Sng'oi in Malaysia, describes his experience with this "earlier" form of consciousness:

Once, while walking [a] steep and very narrow
trail.... I had an almost disabling sinus headache.
Each step pounded in my head. As I trudged up the
steep trail, I looked up and saw a plant I did not
know, maybe twenty feet above me on the side of
the cliff. As I looked at the plant, I knew what it
would feel like (hairy, but not stinging), what it
would smell like (aromatic), and I knew that if I
could get even one leaf of that plant, crush it, and
put it in my nose, it would clear my sinuses. A friend
reached up with a long stick and managed to break
off a leaf of the plant. It felt as I knew it would, and
it smelled as I knew it would. I put it in my nose.
It cleared my sinuses, as I knew it would.[8]

This knowing, which flows from the oneness and interconnectedness of the whole world of creation, was for Wolff
an experience of awakening; it was as if, as he describes
it, "a light was lit deep inside of me."

If we are to regain a mutually sustaining relationship
with life and the created world, we too need to reconnect
with this natural knowing, with this direct relationship
based upon oneness. Then the world can share with us
not just the healing power of plants, but the wisdom we
need for our future. It has a latent knowledge of how to
heal much of its pollution and ecological imbalance. The
earth has many other secrets waiting to be revealed, for
example, how the deep rhythms of life affect the individual and how our consciousness can work in developing
and changing the archetypal patterns of life. But it needs
our conscious cooperation in order to communicate with
us. The earth understands the pivotal role the consciousness of the individual has to play in its evolution. It needs
us to cooperate with the energy that is coming from its
core, with the light that is being awakened.

WELCOMING THE LIGHT

As the light of the world begins now to awaken, our first task is to welcome it into the world. Simple as it seems, this is a very important step. We know in our own inner process the difference between an inner energy that is welcomed into our life and one that is rejected. Rejected energy comes in through the shadow, often violently and destructively breaking into our conscious life. Energy that is accepted can be creatively integrated and give us new life. Its regenerative potential can flow with a minimum of resistance, so that life can once again recreate itself.

In order to welcome it without evoking resistance, we will need to recognize that the energy of this awakened light, which is the energy of life itself, has a very different vibration from that of the patterns of our present existence and structures of consciousness. It belongs to the oneness of life rather than to patterns of separation, and it moves more quickly than our present thought-forms. It is alive in a new way. It does not follow the accepted rules by which we have defined our surface life. And it also has a darkness and density, because it carries the instinctual energy of life itself. It is not split into two, into light and dark, good and bad. It *is*. This energy *is* life awake. We will need to be awake ourselves to be able to welcome in something so unfamiliar and new.

This is a task for each of us individually. Collective consciousness cannot directly welcome what is new, because by its very nature the collective follows what is already defined. Individual consciousness does not need to be so constricted. Its nature is freer and more adaptable; it can change more quickly. This is particularly true of consciousness that has been trained by spiritual practices not to identify, not to be attached, but to acknowledge the transitory nature of all appearances. This allows an individual consciousness to be present with what is new, what is coming into being.

When it is truly welcomed—when we bring this life energy into communion with our individual consciousness—the undefined energy of life can flow into forms that are most beneficial, into images of life that support the whole of life, including both physical life and the life of the soul. It is essential in the next stage of our evolution that the forms into which life flows—the images of life—both benefit our physical existence and nourish the soul. The inner and outer worlds need to come together in a way that is mutually sustaining. There is no need for the inclusion of the soul to work to the detriment of the body, as the past era of duality has seemed to imply. We need not return to an era of physical deprivation, of hunger, and disease: life can be, as Yeats has it, a "blossoming or dancing where/ The body is not bruised to pleasure soul."[9] There is an inherent harmony in life that can bring the two into balance so that they each support and sustain the other. This is a central attribute of the newly awakening energy of life that is waiting for us to welcome it in.

Our individual consciousness is needed in the creation of these new images that will support the whole of life. New images of life are born into our consciousness through the interaction of the energy awakening in the world and our individual consciousness. This is how it has always been at the dawn of a new era. The undifferentiated energy from the core of life needs our individual consciousness in order to create the new forms of living, the new ways of being.

Those attuned to what is really happening can directly participate in this rebirth. On our individual journey we learn to welcome new energy that comes from within and to help it to creatively redefine our life. This often means giving up old patterns of behavior, old self-images. It may mean changing a career or a relationship that inhibits our growth rather than allowing us to be nourished. As we welcome in this new life energy of the whole, we will need to prepare for changes on a much wider scale: at this time of global transition many collective patterns will need to be left behind or transformed. But in keeping with the nature of the energy that is coming in, we will need to allow this change to come from an organic relationship to life and from an interaction of inner and outer. These changes cannot be imposed or forced. Enough damage has been done in the last centuries through the imposing of beliefs or patterns of behavior.

Life needs to recreate itself through us. This is part of our responsibility as guardians of the planet. But in order to work with us, life needs our individual consciousness to have already made the step from separation to oneness—it requires a consciousness that knows that it is part of the whole and does not isolate or protect itself from the prospect of change. The contracting dynamic of self-protection easily distorts what is new into images that threaten its preservation; it does not allow new energy to flow. Once we acknowledge that we are a part of life, that our spark of consciousness is part of the consciousness of the whole of life, then we can be present in a new way where life is coming into being. The light of the world can communicate directly with our individual consciousness and together they can recreate life.

PATTERNS OF RESISTANCE

What is it that holds us back from this simple acknowledgment that we belong to the whole of life? Is it too threatening to our belief in our own individuality to know that we can directly participate in the recreation of life? Would we rather go on blaming others, or corporations or governments, for our present predicament? Is such real democracy too demanding? Or is it our simple fear of leaving behind what we know that makes us choose to stay with our own negative dynamics, our self-destructive patterns, just because they are familiar? We constrict ourselves for so many reasons, and justify ourselves with excuses or intentions for change that we never get around to living.

Life is dying and it needs our light in order to recreate itself. Without the participation of individual consciousness, the images of life as a self-sustaining whole that are needed for its survival cannot be born in time to allow it to recreate itself in the light of its real purpose. On its own, nature evolves too slowly; in the cycles of nature, centuries or millennia of devastation or stagnation in which life-forms contract usually follow upon a major disaster or imbalance. And the ways that human consciousness in the past has aided in the evolution of life are not adapted to the urgent task that faces us now. Human consciousness needs to make a shift into a global dimension; as individuals we need to become conscious of the relationship of our light to the light of the whole and to discover our own direct access to it through the oneness of which we are each a manifestation. We need to begin to take individual responsibility for the light of the planet if the energy that can take us to the next stage of evolution is to be made available to life. This new energy can only be fully born through a relationship of oneness to oneness, of microcosm to macrocosm. The conscious recognition that we each are the life and light of the whole is the catalyst that is needed to make this happen.

This conscious recognition is like a spark between the individual and the whole that can ignite the light of the whole, awaken it to its higher purpose. Without this spark the evolution of the whole will continue—the patterns of globalization are already in place—but there will be no conscious awareness of its real purpose. Instead of moving to the next level of its evolution, life could move backward, into another dark age in which the soul of humanity goes into eclipse. We can continue in our present materialistic self-indulgence for a few more decades; we can continue to develop new technologies for our pleasure and profit. But without the spark between our individual light and the light of the whole, essentially nothing new can be born. Our collective existence will function more and more on a purely physical level. As the images and symbols that are needed to creatively connect the worlds continue to go unformed, our soul will become more and more divorced from our physical life. We will collectively forget why we are here.

One of the secrets of life is that it always recreates itself in the simplest way. Life is a living organism of which we are a part. The center of our being is at the center of life. In our thoughts and imaginings we may perceive ourself as alienated or at the periphery of life, but that is only another illusion.

Life is an expression of the divine and we each hold the light of the divine within our own heart. Part of spiritual practice is to affirm this inner reality with each and every breath, and so to affirm the connection of love that is at the core of life. If we forget this, we lose our conscious affirmation of the simple essence that is the divine presence within ourself and within life. It is this simple essence that is recreating itself—the divine being reborn in a new way within ourself and within life. The work of the lover is to be fully present at this mystery of rebirth, to be alive to His need to use us as He makes Himself known to Himself in a new way.

At first all that is needed is for us to be aware that our light is part of the light of the whole and to allow a relationship between the two lights—to welcome the light of the whole into the world. Through this relationship we will be drawn into a creative network of light that supports the creation of new forms and the energy that is needed to sustain them. How this relationship of light to light will develop depends upon a number of factors, such as how much resistance from the collective it encounters, and how hard the collective and its old ways will fight for their survival. Certain constellations of worldly power can adapt to accommodate what is being born while others are too constrictive to allow any new light to enter. Some negative patterns can be worked around, while others may have to be directly confronted.

We can be individually aligned with the forces of creation. This is the opportunity this moment in history offers us: we can bring our light into relationship with what is being born. It is a simple affirmation of our own power and the power of life. And there is a quality of joy in this: once again life is recreating itself and we are a part of this recreation. We are a part of the light of God being manifest in a new way.

3.

CONSCIOUSNESS
AND CHANGE

A tsunami, a typhoon, a cyclone,
an earthquake are not disasters,
they are natural phenomena.
A human being unable to reach out,
his humanity unexpressed, divinity unattained
is the disaster.

Sadhguru Jaggi Vasudev

OUR CONSCIOUSNESS
CAN RECREATE THE WORLD

The earth is changing. The living being that is our world
is undergoing a metamorphosis, a transformation of its
inner essence, as something within the core of its being
comes alive. And we are a part of this change. It may seem
to us that we live on the surface of the world, sustaining
ourselves from a thin topsoil that is becoming ever more
degraded. But this is just an appearance, a manifestation
of the myth of the previous era that viewed humanity as
separate from the world it inhabits. In fact a human being
is part of the essential nature of creation; our consciousness is part of the consciousness of the world. And because
of this we influence the patterns of creation, the archetypal energies that define our existence, much more than
we know.

Our collective myths are more than a story we tell
ourselves about the world—they shape the way we live in

it, and even more fundamentally affect how the energy of life itself can flow. The myth of the past era gave rise to the idea of science as a purely objective pursuit and allowed us to believe we could impose our will upon the natural world. This has become such a dominant view of our world that we have even forgotten that it is a myth, a product of our consciousness. As a result, though we may see the connection between our actions and the pollution and ecological imbalance that are sickening the world, we fail to see the underlying cause, the myth that has made those actions appear logical and acceptable, and so we cannot trace our situation to its real source: our consciousness. It is our consciousness that has created this ailing world.

Spiritual teachings tell us that our attitude creates our world; if we change inwardly, change our thought-patterns and attitudes, our world will change. We interpret this to mean that *our experience* of the world will change, as in fact it does when we become more detached, less caught in anxiety or desire. Some "new-age" teachings go further, suggesting that we can change our outer circumstances—that we can manifest our dreams or desires, attract what we want, and so be happier and more successful, make our world more personally agreeable. But we understand these ideas only within a personal frame of reference: how our attitude affects our individual life. We have not taken the radical step of realizing that our consciousness is a creative and determining force in all of creation. But this is the truth to which we are about to awaken. This is the real meaning of being a co-creator in the world. We do not just create our own world, or our own experience of the world. Our consciousness, particularly consciousness that is spiritually awake, is central to recreating the whole world.

Of course on the surface we can look around and see the world we have created, the changes we have wrought on the natural systems of the planet—the forests we have cut down, the plains we have ploughed up and built upon, the natural waterways we have diverted to create our cities and farmlands; the delicately balanced ecosystems we have forever altered to accommodate our industries; the ravages of war. We are even becoming aware that our activities have changed the climate, contributing to global warming, drought, acid rain. But we do not yet realize that we have affected the very life force of the planet; we do not comprehend the way the primal energies of creation manifest. We have not understood the real relationship between our consciousness and the planet or taken responsibility for that relationship.

As we step into an era of global awareness, we know that the world is very different from what it was even a few decades ago. Through the media and the Internet we can instantly know, with unprecedented immediacy, what is happening around the planet; we can see its images with our own eyes, hear its sounds and voices. We can respond to a disaster in one part of the world with prayers or material support almost as soon as it happens. Our collective consciousness can now be aligned to what is happening on the whole planet. But we have not yet taken the next step, which is to realize that it is not happening to somebody else; it is all happening to us. There is no "over there" any more. When the terrorists hit the World Trade Center, everyone was affected, and the prayers that came in response came from around the whole world. The tsunami in 2005 touched us all, either physically or in our hearts and compassion. Yet we have not fully grasped what this means, what this new awareness is telling us: that the consciousness of humanity is one consciousness and is a part of life itself, and that this step into global awareness belongs to the consciousness of the world as it comes alive in a new way—that the world is waking up.

When consciousness is awake it behaves very differently from the way it behaves when it is asleep. When we are unconscious, our life is a continuous repetition of patterns, the same dream repeated in endless variations, with little growth or real change. One knows in one's own life how patterns of relationship—dynamics of conflict—keep recurring; the scenarios may change, but the basic patterns remain the same. (One of the purposes of therapy is to help one to become conscious so that one can change the underlying patterns.) What is true for the individual is true for the whole. The collective dreams that we live when we are asleep change only gradually over centuries. How many wars have been fought, how many women raped? So little has changed even now. We may live in more comfortable homes, travel in cars rather than on horses, but the instincts that dominate us are largely the same; we follow similar desires and fantasies, get caught in similar jealousies and petty hatreds. We are driven by the same forces, which we hardly understand and cannot control.

But what would happen if we woke up to the awareness that our consciousness and our life force are part of the consciousness and life force of the planet, and that there is a direct relationship between the individual and the whole? If we awoke to the simple truth that nothing is separate, nothing is "over there" any more? At present we are fighting this awareness, taking refuge in insularity, in the divisive forces of race and religious sectarianism, tribalism, and nationalism, in the drive to dominate others whether through force or through trade. We are trying to remain asleep. But we cannot stop this awakening awareness of the whole. We can only miss its meaning and the opportunity contained in it. And if we do, we will not be able to participate in this change.

THE RELATIONSHIP BETWEEN
INDIVIDUAL CONSCIOUSNESS AND THE WORLD

The relationship between our consciousness and the consciousness of the world is on one level quite simple: human consciousness *is* the higher consciousness of the world. When the spark of divine consciousness was given to the first humans, it was given to the world. We carry the higher consciousness of life. Animals carry a different consciousness, an instinctual awareness that is naturally part of the wholeness of life. It follows different laws from those of human consciousness, and does not have the same potential for higher evolution. When an animal dies, its life force returns to the life force of the planet; an animal cannot evolve outside of its physical body. The soul of a human being, which is not limited to the physical world, can evolve and grow beyond death. And because we carry the higher consciousness of life, this higher evolution affects the evolution of the world.

The arrival of human consciousness was a big step in planetary evolution, and the development of human consciousness has been central to the development of the planet. With our narrow cultural focus on the outer material world, we are unaware of this; we tend to see progress in material terms. But the true measure of a civilization are not the monuments it leaves behind, its sciences or the sophistication of its weapons or the standard of living its citizens enjoy, but the quality of the consciousness it fosters. The real evolution is the evolution of consciousness. And the next step in planetary evolution requires that we wake up to the central role that consciousness plays in it, and that we recognize our consciousness as a part of the consciousness of the whole and step into the awareness and responsibility that brings.

Consciousness is a creative force. We often associate consciousness with the mind, not realizing that while consciousness often works *through* the mind, it is much more than our mental activities, more than our constantly recycling thought-patterns. In fact people who live unconsciously are most easily caught in the mind's endless repetitions: they do not have direct access to the creative aspect of consciousness that is a dynamic agent of change. It can be instructive to watch one's mind and see how much of the thinking process is actually a creative response to a situation and how much is simply recycled, from conditioning, memories, or impressions from others. Consciousness can even be a threat to the mind itself, which likes to be in control and has endless strategies, like keeping us preoccupied with anxiety-inducing images and thoughts, to keep us from freely responding to the moment.

Awakened consciousness is alive to the moment, not simply following conditioned patterns. Consciousness uses the mind to gather and assimilate information and to express itself, but it is only alive when it is responding in the moment. Sometimes one can watch a conflict within oneself between a conditioned reaction, with its secure feeling of familiarity, and the vulnerability and insecurity of a real conscious response. It is always easier to be asleep, more dangerous to be awake. Asleep, we know our dreams and even our demons all too well. Awake, one does not know what will happen.

Spiritual practices teach one to be awake, to be free from conditioning, to be present and alive to the real need of the moment. This is one of the reasons that spiritual consciousness is so important at this time of global change. As the whole world is going through this transition, it needs the participation of consciousness that is not caught in the patterns of the past but is awake and alert to each moment to help to facilitate this creative shift.

Consciousness is a spark of the divine that we bring from the plane of the soul into the physical world. It is a connection between the inner and outer worlds, and in its innermost core it carries a remembrance of our origin, of our divine source. Without this remembrance something essential to life is lost: life's real purpose goes unrecognized. We are here to bring the awareness of the divine into this world, to witness Him in His world. This is the primordial covenant, which we agreed to before human beings came into creation, when the not-yet-created humanity was asked "Am I not your Lord?" and they replied, "Yes, we witness it." This act of witnessing was and is done for the sake of the Creator and for the whole of His creation. Witnessing Him in His world fulfills a primal purpose of creation, the purpose expressed in the *hadîth* "I was a hidden treasure and I longed to be known, so I created the world."

On this level our consciousness *is* the world con-sciously remembering God. And any conscious act or state of awareness that carries this quality of remembrance is a direct reflection of the light of the divine in this world. It is a light in the world that looks towards God. When the medieval sculptors created the images for the cathedrals they were praising God. When Bach composed his cantatas he was praising God. Their creativity was a light looking towards God, and when we are open to their art, we too are turned towards Him. We are part of their prayer and praise, just as, more hiddenly, we are part of the prayer of every supplicant who opens her heart to God, or of the longing of any lover whose heart cries for her Beloved. The light that comes from these offerings sustains the whole world. This light *is* the world looking towards God, *is* the world being aware of its divine nature.

The moment we turn our attention towards the divine, we are the light of the world returning to God. Our consciousness is a spark of divine light fulfilling its purpose. And this spark is not something abstract; it is not a spiritual idea but a living, dynamic light that is fully alive. Nor is it something separate from life: it is life itself expressing its divine nature, witnessing God. When we recognize this, we find that we are connected to the core of life, to the light that is within creation. The simple act of remembrance and awareness places us at the very center of life. We are honoring and fulfilling life's divine nature.

As a dynamic center of light, consciousness is continually changing, just as life itself is constantly changing. Any attempt to keep consciousness fixed results in stagnation. Consciousness is more dynamic than our thinking patterns or attitudes or behavior, and it is often seen as a threat to established order, whether in the individual or in the collective. To be consciously alive means to be present only to the reality of the moment, knowing that everything is in continual flux. Real wisdom lies in knowing how to work with this flux, with the patterns or energy structures that belong to the dynamics of change. The Chinese sages understood that if we are to live close to the Source we need to understand these changes, a wisdom that found expression in the *I Ching: The Book of Changes*. In our culture we prefer the illusion of a life that is as fixed and defined as possible—we have been conditioned to be cautious, even threatened by change. We still inhabit a Newtonian universe, a predictable world ruled by fixed laws. We have not yet dared to imagine a world that arises moment by moment out of dynamic energies acting not according to fixed laws but to shifting patterns of probability, which science now tells us is nearer to the truth.

To live consciously means to step out of a defined vision of the world into a dynamic interplay of forces and events. It does not mean to abandon order for chaos, but to recognize that order is not something fixed; it is instead a way to live in harmony with what is real. Rather than imposing a belief or system on life, one becomes present in life's flux, witnessing and experiencing it as a constantly changing expression of divine oneness—and the closer one lives to one's own divine nature, the faster the experience of change becomes.

Within these changes there are patterns and probabilities, patterns that belong to the way the divine expresses itself in the world. We see them expressed in the geometric proportions of nature; they also underlie the Gothic cathedral sculptures and stained glass designs, and Bach's cantatas. These patterns are also changing and evolving now, as the way the divine expresses itself in the world is changing, and it is our ability to understand and work with them that enables us to be a creative partner in life.

How can we live consciously within our present culture that has no knowledge of these patterns—that has imposed itself upon the natural world and the natural order and uses power and will to uphold its values and way of life with no regard for what is happening to the planet? In fact our contemporary culture uses most of its energy and power to protect its way of life. It works against, rather than with, the changes taking place. It has no awareness that these changes are themselves following patterns, rhythms within life. Yet our collective blindness is also part of life— we retreat into our blindness just as a threatened animal retreats within its lair, draws back into its shell, or curls, like a hedgehog, into a ball of prickles. Our resistance to change is part of these larger patterns of change.

To live consciously in our present world means to accept what is happening, both the changes and the resistance. It is unconsciousness that retreats into a dream of denial. Consciousness has access to an ancient wisdom, a knowing that the primal forces of life, always moving, always flowing, will find their way. Returning to the Source, we will find a power within life that is stronger than any pattern of resistance, an energy whose suppleness will overcome what is rigid and fixed. Our work is to remain with this primal energy of life, to align our consciousness with its flow. Then we will find that we are a part of life recreating itself. Everything, even our culture's collective denial, is a part of this unfolding pattern. Life is darkness and light and all the spectrum of shadows between. We are this whole spectrum of life, the denial and the affirmation, the memory and the moment. Paradoxically, even our longing for stability is part of a pattern of change: if there were no change there would be no desire for stability. Our ignorance is simply the denial of life and its divine, constantly changing nature. Our awakening is the knowing that all is One. Once we live this awakened awareness, we can work with the patterns of creation, rather than trying to fight the forces of denial.

The forces of denial are all around us, in the corporations and hierarchies of power that appear to dominate and determine our collective life. Their profit motives drive the mechanisms of much of our civilization. It is easy to think that we live in their shadow or under their power. They have a life-denying energy, and if we try to fight them inwardly or outwardly we will find ourselves in a dark web that drains much of our energy and light. But the wasteland they have created is an aspect of a contraction that happens at the end of any era, when the life energy withdraws from the old forms. It is essential that we also withdraw our consciousness from this dying dream, that we give our light to what is being born.

Yet these structures constantly attract our attention, either with the glamour of their seductive illusions or the drama of the problems they create. Our consciousness is drawn away from the essential simplicity of life into complexities that create more complexity. How often do we lose the thread of what is essential to life in this sticky web we live in now that we call everyday life? If we look closely we will see that much of our life energy is wasted, devoured by the demands of this corporate monster that has us continually on hold.

We need to make an effort to return our attention to life itself. There are simple practices of awareness that can help. Awareness of breath is a most basic practice that turns our attention back to what is essential. Simple acts of loving kindness towards others also reconnect us with the real web of life, the genuine interconnections between people. Learning to walk in a sacred manner, the Native American practice of walking with a conscious aware-ness of placing one's foot on the sacred earth, is a way of bringing one's attention back to the sacred nature of the world. The "Practice of the Presence of God" described by Brother Lawrence,[1] in which one does one's daily actions in God's company (Brother Lawrence, working in the kitchen, peeled the potatoes with God, washed the carrots with God) until He becomes a constant presence, reaffirms the divine in daily life.

Ours is not a simple culture. It demands much of our energy and consciousness just to get by. But life itself is simple, and when we consciously reconnect with this essential quality, we will find that we are nourished rather than drained. And our consciousness will also nourish life; our light will give life an energy it needs in order to change and transform. The light of individual consciousness is a catalyst in the awakening of the primal energy of life.

And as we return our awareness to life, we will discover that our consciousness becomes attuned to the patterns within life and the way that life is changing. We will find that these patterns, these inner dynamics, are quite different from the forces that appear to govern our outer life, and they can work in harmony with us. They belong to the way life is evolving, and can evolve through us. We are a secret ingredient in life's evolution, because we carry the consciousness of life's divine oneness. This simple but essential awareness is needed by life.

All around us we can see that life is one. We are living in an interconnected world in which nothing is separate and everything is interdependent. This awareness is essential to life. We are distracted and deceived by the idea that we are living in a complex world that requires complex solutions to its problems. This is true only if we forget that the world is one living being. Once we recognize that it is one and we bring this awareness back into life, then life can respond as one living being, rather than as a complex problem. Our consciousness helps to create the paradigm within which the world can come alive.

CREATING A RELATIONSHIP
WITH THE ARCHETYPAL WORLD

In previous eras people were more naturally aligned with the primal forces within life. The cycles of nature aligned those who worked with the land, while other everyday activities, like preparing food, had a ritual quality that attuned those involved in them to life's sacred rhythms. Reverence for the gods of the hearth and the home had a similar function, as did the many rituals and celebrations that were a part of the cycle of life. What later became labeled as superstition or paganism was in fact a way to live in harmony with the primal patterns of life, the rhythms of its energy.

Now we need to reclaim a harmony with the forces within life. We cannot go back to an agricultural way of life or a world ruled by ritual; those outer forms have lost their deeper meaning. But now we know that these primal patterns and rhythms, which earlier societies revered as their gods, are archetypal forces, and that they exist within our own psyche. In order to reclaim the harmony we have lost, we need to reconnect with these forces within ourselves.

To do this, we need to acknowledge them and make a conscious relationship with them, one founded upon respect and understanding. Then we will discover that our consciousness can directly communicate with these energies within life: we can enter into a new relationship with these ancient gods. This is not an imposed relationship, forced upon us by priests demanding sacrifices. It is a simple and natural honoring of the truth that we are all a part of life and need to work and live together, in both the inner and outer worlds. The archetypes need our conscious cooperation just as we need their power if we are to redeem the world. To be a co-creator with life is to reclaim a way of working with the powers of the inner world, to understand their patterns and rhythms.

Once we step outside of the framework of our mind and ego, we will find ourselves in a world in which many different forces are at work, forces outside the scope of our reasoning minds. We have been conditioned to fear what we cannot rationally understand. But our rational approach to the world is a fairly recent development; it is not deeply rooted in our consciousness, however tight its grip may feel or however useful it may be to the structures of worldly power. If previous cultures knew how to live in relationship with the inner world, why should we deny ourselves this opportunity? We need not be frightened of the powers within life, though we rightly hold them in awe, as we would the force of an earthquake or hurricane. If we treat them with respect, we can learn how to live with them in a creative and mutually beneficial way.

We have seen how this can work on our individual journey, how through dance, dreaming, art, inner dialogue or other means we find our own way into the inner world and learn how to relate to its inhabitants. We discover how the inner healer, for example, gives us wisdom, how the warrior gives us strength. Through these inner figures we may gain access to new creativity or inner power, or find a balance and harmony that come from within. We may discover new doors opening in our own lives, new and unexpected opportunities, new ways of living. But we also become aware that these energies are not just a part of our personal psyche, affecting just our own life, but that they belong to all of life—that working with these powers within us we are working with the whole.

What we may not realize is that through our own communion with the inner world we are creating a new way for the gods to relate to man: not through shamans, priests or imposed rituals, but through the individual. In the interconnected oneness of life we are building a bridge between the worlds for the whole of humanity. Individually and together we are creating a connection, a relationship with life's inner forces, through which they can teach us how to live in harmony with them once again. The archetypes themselves can teach us the patterns behind life, and the ways to work with life's primal powers. A knowledge that has been lost can be given back to us, given from the inner world to the outer world of ordinary consciousness. The gods will be able to speak to humanity once again.

What matters in this dialogue is our conscious connection with the inner world, and our respect for the energies we encounter. But we have forgotten the power of the inner worlds, which every other culture has held in reverence. We live in a culture that respects little apart from surface glamour, the trappings of worldly power and material possessions. And we live in the grip of anxieties and fears, which we project onto the outer world as if outer events were the only source of our unease. We do not dare to recognize that what we really fear is the inner world, which we do not know and cannot control—here reside the shadows used by terrorists, and the real powers that shape our lives. The real danger lies in our denial of them, our dismissal of the reality of the inner world.

When we reclaim a conscious relationship with the inner world, we will find that these fears lose their grip on us. We will discover that there are beneficial forces waiting to help us—just as there are beneficial forces within the planet waiting to clear up the pollution, once we learn how to work with them. But we will have to recognize that this is a two-way relationship. We have imposed our beliefs and ideas upon the world for too long. Now we need to work in relationship with life, both in the outer and inner world.

This is why the wisdom of the feminine is so important, because the feminine understands the dynamics of relationship, how to listen and be receptive. Feminine consciousness is more attuned to the life of the body, and so knows the rhythms that belong to the cycles of life, rather than the systems imposed by will that are presently strangling our world. The feminine is more instinctively and naturally attuned to life, its patterns and powers. And feminine consciousness is less dominated by reason, more open to the mystery of the symbolic inner world. The feminine is vital in this work of awakening.

The rhythms and patterns are within us and within life. We just need to be open and receptive to uncover them, to listen to what the inner and outer worlds are waiting to communicate. This is something so simple it is easily overlooked, but it also places upon each one of us the responsibility for the future. No one is here to tell us how it is going to be; it is for each of us to discover. Through our individual conscious relationship with the world the future will be born.

CONSCIOUSNESS AS A CATALYST

In this work consciousness is the catalyst. Consciousness *is* the connection between the outer and inner, the individual and the whole, that is needed to spark life's awakening. Without it nothing new can be born. But with the light of our consciousness, the patterns within life and within ourselves can begin to change and come alive in a new way. The archetypal shifts that happen gradually over centuries can be speeded up. These primal forces can help us resolve the global problems we have created, and together we can discover a new way to be with ourselves and with life. We can create a civilization based upon oneness and interrelatedness.

Just because we have forgotten how to work with life's energy does not mean that it is inaccessible, or that it is not waiting to be used. Once we step outside of the isolated image of our individual self, we will find that we are part of an organic restructuring of life in which our consciousness is being realigned with the energy within life. We will begin to awaken to the light that is waking up within the world, to the life that is waking up within and around us. We will have to be attentive: the signs of this shift—which are barely visible in any case as what is awakening is so new—may be all the more difficult to see through the dense clouds of materialism and forgetfulness we presently live in. But if we are attentive, each in our own way we will start to feel these changes, in subtle ways and perhaps more potently as well, as we become attuned to them.

We may sense it first in a hope that was not there before, a feeling of being closer to life, being part of the whole of humanity in a different way. Then we will sense the feeling of isolation, of alienation from life, beginning to dissolve and a deep sense of purpose beginning to surface, a knowing that we are working together with each other and with the world. Of course any time of crisis can evoke this shared purpose, bringing people selflessly together to help one other. What will be different now is that we will sense we are working together with the world itself, with its very life force—at this time of crisis, it is the world that needs our help. It needs the commitment of our consciousness as we give our light, this gift of consciousness we have been given, back to life. To work in this way will involve a simple realignment of our everyday consciousness, a quality of attention or awareness that was not there before. Our outer circumstances may not change much. But the difference we will experience, that comes from being consciously connected to the whole and to the way the whole is changing, will be fundamental and profound. And it will be life's gift back to us.

When we make the commitment of our consciousness to the world, when we give our light to its light, the archetypal energies within life can begin to shift the shapes that dominate our collective consciousness, and give us new images and dreams that are more self-sustaining. These new images and patterns are already constellating beneath the surface; some people are already tuned into them. But it will take an influx of energy to enable these creative forces to break through the constrictive patterns of resistance that belong to the darkness of greed, fear, and self-interest that at present drives our collective. The energy needed for this breakthrough is already within the world, hidden within its energy centers. These energy centers are waiting to be unlocked so that their power can be used for this transition. The keys to unlock them are particular qualities or energies of consciousness. For example, the mystical consciousness that looks only towards God, that remembers Him in His world, is one such key. This is why individuals and groups of mystics have been positioned at certain places in the inner and outer worlds in order to facilitate this work of unlocking the centers of power.

Different centers function in different ways; some have a more local effect while others are global.[2] The way they work is a well-guarded secret, but once they are unlocked they can be activated to different degrees, releasing a corresponding amount of energy, similar to the way that the psychic centers or *chakras* in an individual can become activated to different degrees. In an individual the energy released from the *chakras* speeds up her spiritual evolution and can help give her access to different levels of consciousness. But the energy must be released in the right degree and at the right time if it is not to unbalance the individual, which is why at a certain point on the journey one needs to put oneself in the hands of a master.

The different energy centers in the world also need to be unlocked with care. They need to work together in harmony so that the energy structure of the world remains in balance. This is one of the reasons that spiritual masters in different parts of the world are working together inwardly: so that the evolution of the world can be balanced. There are also safeguards in place preventing the misuse of the centers of power. Part of the esoteric knowledge of the future will be a greater understanding of how these centers work, so that we can use their energy in the most beneficial way.

On all levels life is attracting those whose consciousness it needs to help in this work of global transformation. To some it is speaking directly to their souls; they feel its cry within their hearts or in their dreams. Others it is attracting through their outer life, drawing them to participate creatively in areas of work that are beneficial to the planet. Some people are apparently working or praying alone, while many experience being linked together, connected to a network of people helping the world to awaken. What is central is to realize that we are each being called into a new relationship with life and the planet. An openness to this relationship and an appreciation of its importance will enable us to participate most fully, to become creatively engaged in this work. Creativity is always a relationship.

Those who are drawn to this work need to remember that it is life itself that has called us. This is not some spiritual ideal. This is life itself in its need to survive and evolve: it could not be more simple or essential. In order to change, it is attracting our consciousness, reminding us of an ancient pledge and awakening us to the global dimension of our own ordinary self.

4.

IMAGES OF LIFE

Those images that yet
Fresh images beget.

W. B. Yeats[1]

THE VEILS OF CREATION

The veils of creation, the images of the world, hold us in their subtle grasp. These images, depicting our world, create the reality within which we mostly live. If we stop and look, we can see some of the images that shape our individual lives—the images we have of ourself, created by the ego or given to us by our parents, often quite at variance with our real nature; and our images of the outer world, our projections and attachments, and the seductive images of our desires. Some hold us with their promises of fulfillment or happiness. Others attract us more subversively, with problems or difficulties that draw us into their dark web. Yet others project a sense of purpose into our lives. Through these images we define our individual lives, or are defined by them.

We are also held within the veils of our collective conditioning: our shared images and beliefs, the values that delineate our collective life—for example our collective goals and our images of success or failure, our images of marriage and family life, and other patterns of social behavior. For some there are also the veils of religious belief, the sacred images and codes of behavior that give meaning or hold us through guilt. For others the veils take the form of more socially-defined values, like justice or equality, or the siren of material prosperity.

Most of the images that fill our minds and define our world are created by our conscious or unconscious self or by the power of the collective. But today many images are also purposefully crafted by the corporations that need us to consume their products. These are the images that attract our attention. We are besieged and overrun by these manufactured images of self-indulgence, which imprison us not only in the cycle of desire but also more and more in financial debt, holding us both inwardly and outwardly in their thrall—the image of material prosperity has a demonic side, though we barely even notice it, so skillfully is it manipulated in our advertising culture.

Through these myriad veils we create our life and define our progress within its maze. We may change some of our images, create different desires, refocus on certain values and reject others; we may even take steps to resist the seductive images of advertising and the media. But we rarely recognize them for the dream they are, and we live and die within the dream. We have almost forgotten that there are other images that come not from our self-created world but from higher worlds. These images do not hold us confined within our self-created dream but rather reconnect us to our source; they remind us of our real Self and our Creator. Nature in its beauty and power is the most obvious example of a created image that calls us back to our source, and many of us turn to it to find what may be missing in the rest of our lives. We may find that its outer stillness resonates with a longing for inner stillness, or that its power stirs memories of a greater power. We might experience in nature that a veil can fall away and allow us to glimpse what is behind and within our transitory world:

> a sense sublime
> Of something far more deeply interfused,
> Whose dwelling is the light of setting suns,
> And the round ocean and the living air,
> And the blue sky, and in the mind of man.[2]

But our present Western world lives far from nature, and even the power of the natural world often cannot overcome the soul-denying images of our everyday life, images that consume our energy rather than nourish us. And in a world created by these images, we have very little else to reconnect us to our source.

In traditional cultures this was not the case. Along with a greater closeness to the natural world, the images and symbols of myth, sacred art, architecture, music, dance, and ritual also served to remind people of the divine, to connect them with humanity's real roots. An image like the hero or the crone could give an archetypal dimension to an ordinary life, while sacred buildings, such as a Gothic cathedral, could show people their symbolic place in the world and its relation to the divine. These ancient images have persisted into our modern era, but we have forgotten how to keep them alive, how to recreate them anew out of our own deepest experience, to keep them feeding their meaning into our everyday lives. Instead we have replaced the potency of the creative imagination with the transitory play of fantasies that have no symbolic depth. As a secular society, we have only the fragmented remnants of those past cultures in which the images of the creative imagination and myth and art functioned as sacred mediators that nourished the soul. The daily rituals of today's hurried existence have long lost any connection to the sacred dimension of life.

Instead we are caught in a self-destructive cycle, unable ecologically to sustain the images of material prosperity by which we define our life. These images are destroying our planet and we go on about our daily lives, mostly oblivious to what is happening. Is there a way to change these images? Is there a way to work *with* the veils of creation, instead of being cut off and trapped inside them?

FREEDOM FROM THE IMAGES THAT BIND

Behind the veils of creation a very different dance is taking place. Here there are no images to define us, no forms that constrict our eternal nature. Here is the energy of life in its undiluted nature, the primal power of creation before it is captured in images. Here light and love flow without effort, and joy is present. This is the realm of pure being and the simplicity of what *is*. Here is the realm of the higher mind, the part of our consciousness that does not create images or desires but exists in its own purity and higher intention.

Much of the work on the spiritual path is to free ourself from desires and attachments, to recognize the images created by our ego and our collective conditioning and say, "I am not this." On the Sufi path this work belongs to the stage of *fanâ*, annihilation; it is a painful process that undermines or destroys all the images that bind us, until only the One remains. We live the truth that "Everything perishes except His face." With the sword of spiritual discrimination we cut away the attachments of the world, and through the practice of meditation we train the mind not to continually create new images and desires. Then maybe for an instant we step behind the veils of this world into another dimension that appears empty and silent. To a consciousness that knows only form, this emptiness can at first be frightening, its silence overwhelming. But gradually, as we become familiar with this undefined world, we awaken to a very different quality of life, a world of pure being and pure consciousness. We discover that in this dimension we exist free of any conditioning and as our real Self.

And so the journey continues and the horizons expand. We see the limitations of form and yet come to know its purpose; we see how through form the one light of pure being becomes scattered into colors to reflect back the light in a myriad of ways. We see the wonder and terror of creation, not as its victim or prisoner, but as a free human being who knows its transient, ever-changing nature. And with this freedom we are able to participate in life as it really is. Because life is not just a collection of images and desires. It is not just a dream or a nightmare. It is not just a myriad of discordant impressions, but a unified whole, the manifestation of a light that has a divine purpose. But this reality can only be recognized from outside the veils of creation. In the words of St. Paul, "For now we see through a glass, darkly; but then face to face: now I know in part; but then shall I know even as I am known."

What does it mean to participate in life as it really is? It means to be present at the core of creation, at the place of pure being, while at the same time being immersed in life's images. We are the thread of creation that links the worlds together. We are the light and the darkness, the laughter and the tears; we hold all the images within us. As human beings we have the unique capacity to know that it is all one. We hold in our hearts the love that links us to the Creator, a love that calls forth His creation and asks us to witness it. In the heart of His lover His oneness is revealed, His secret face made visible: our Beloved makes Himself known to us and to His world, and we see that everything is He. His lovers know all of life's images as reflections of Him whom we love.

Traditionally the ones who have passed through the veils of creation stand detached from the world, watching its comings and goings, acting, in the words of Shakespeare's King Lear, as "God's spies." The mystical wayfarer often plays this part. Being "in the world but not of the world," he is the "eyes and ears of God." He looks upon the world awake to its real mystery. He has the compassion born of true detachment, and though he may laugh at human folly, he can also feel sorrow that so many are caught in painful illusions, their light hidden from them.

But there are times when a real need arises for those not constricted by any form, belief, or ideology to participate in life in order to create new images, new ways of being. Then the mystic becomes like a midwife of the imagination, bringing forth images that can heal and restore. Now is such a time. The world needs the images of its future or it will die. It needs images born from the beyond, not resurrected from the debris of the past. It needs images that have the power to free us from the grip of consumerism and give us hope, images that cannot be manipulated by the corporate forces of greed that control so much of our present world. It needs images that speak to what is highest within humanity and yet are grounded in everyday reality.

IMAGES FOR OUR FUTURE

Some of these images have already been given to us: images of global oneness and interconnectivity. When the first astronaut saw the world as a single sphere without frontiers, humanity was given a new image of living wholeness. And now the Internet has given us a world-wide web of interconnections, though we have yet to understand the full implications of these emerging patterns of relationship. The discoveries of particle physics have also given us an awareness of matter that can free us from the mechanical images of the Newtonian worldview, new images of a reality in which consciousness, energy, and matter are interdependent. These are all stepping-stones to a new world that is being born around us.

Another emerging image that connects us directly with the whole is the image of man as microcosm. This image used to be a part of our symbolic consciousness, and its potency can still be seen in Leonardo's drawing of a man with arms outstretched inside a square-within-a-circle, the circle and square symbolizing the union of heaven and earth that man embodies. The image of man as microcosm belongs also to the alchemical tradition and to Sufism, which describes the relationship of the individual to the whole as that of the small Adam, the human being, to the greater Adam, the cosmos in its entirety. The importance of the image of man as microcosm to our present time is that it gives the individual a direct relationship to the whole world, not via governments, corporations, or other hierarchical structures but within himself. It affirms that our own oneness and the oneness of all of creation are intrinsically connected, and gives the individual more power and potential for transformation than we could have imagined possible in the world created by our present images.

The image of man as microcosm returns the individual to the very center of life. During the era that is now coming to a close, especially in the West we have followed to its extreme the drive to realize our individuality, with the result that we now experience ourselves as fully separate beings. While the extreme development of our individuality may have given us the illusion of individual freedom, choice, and self-expression, its price has been isolation, loneliness, and a deep sense of disconnection from others and from life as a whole. The image of the individual as microcosm does not mean that we lose our sense of individuality, our uniqueness, which is the great gift in the West of the past era, but that we return it to the center of creation and acknowledge our role at the very center of the profound interconnectedness of life.

Symbolic images like the web of life, the world as a living whole, the individual as microcosm are not just images of something, in the way that a photograph is an image. They have a symbolic power and life force that belong to the archetypal world. They exist in the inner world, the *mundus imaginalis* that is the intermediary between the outer world of the senses and the world of pure consciousness. Traditionally, working with such symbols is seen as part of the spiritual ascent, the return from the outer world of forms to their source in the spiritual realm. However, these images also belong to the descent of the energy from the Source into creation. Jung described such images as "the riverbeds of life." Through them the energy of creation flows from the unmanifest world into manifestation. Working with such symbols allows us to participate in this drama of creation, to interact with the forces of life before they are crystallized into the images that define our outer life.

Traditionally this has been the work of the shaman or *magus*, one who has been trained in the power of the symbolic inner world and knows how to work with its images for the benefit of others. Of course this work has always had the potential to be misused, to fall into the hands of those who manipulate the images of the inner world for their own personal gain, to enhance their own personal power. In recent years many of these previously secret techniques have become more widely known, and the danger of misuse has grown accordingly. While it can be beneficial to discover one's power animal and have access to one's inner energy or blocked creativity, the use of the imagination and its symbolic images to fulfill one's dreams—to create the external life one desires—also has its dark side. People who are drawn by discontent or greed into using these ancient techniques rarely recognize that they are using dark magic, that they are bartering their soul for personal gain. Our infatuation with our individual self, our contemporary creed that we have the right to what we want, and our childish reluctance to acknowledge real responsibility for our actions in the outer or inner world have a darker side than we dare to acknowledge. Real shamanic work, like alchemy, is always done for the sake of the whole.

The image of ourselves as the microcosm of the whole firmly reminds us of our relationship and responsibility to the whole of creation, not as an abstract theory but as a living symbolic reality. It also gives us the power to affect the whole more than we realize. This image is alive with the energy of its content; it has the capacity to direct our consciousness towards its own profoundly interconnected nature, its connections to the whole of existence. When we bring it into our own consciousness, we bring it into the consciousness of the whole of humanity. And this awakening consciousness of the whole with all its interconnections can interact in a way our previous era's image of gradual, linear development could never encompass. The way that the Internet and other forms of global communication, for example, have so quickly and vibrantly transformed our lives would have been hard even to imagine twenty years ago.

Yet our collective consciousness has not caught up with these developments. We are still reluctant to fully acknowledge the Internet as the new form of global consciousness it is—a consciousness that cannot be caught in hierarchical power structures or imposed patterns of relationship, that is alive in its own organic way, beyond our ability to control. Already life is beginning to recreate itself on a global pattern of interrelationship, and we do not yet recognize what is happening.

The image of the human being as a microcosm suggests that we each have all of these patterns of relationship within us. As the mediator between the inner and outer worlds, we hold the key to understanding and using the power and life force that are held by these patterns. The traffic on the Internet is not just individuals looking for information, buying goods, or sending e-mails. It is an exchange of consciousness. Along the optic cables that bring this interchange to the world, the light of individual consciousness is flowing, meeting, and interrelating with the light of millions of others. This meeting of consciousness, this interrelationship of light, is life giving birth to itself; it is global consciousness waking up. The individual who recognizes this has the potential to be aligned with its real purpose, and to bring the light of higher consciousness into this human drama.

CONSCIOUSNESS AND
THE LIGHT HIDDEN IN DARKNESS

We are all interconnected and everyone is at the center of this awakening. But the one who knows what is happening has an advantage—he or she is no longer just an unconscious participant. We know on our own inner journey what happens when our individual consciousness interacts with our unconscious patterns: it initiates the alchemical work of liberating the light hidden in darkness. It gives us access to parts of ourself and energies within us that have been hidden or inaccessible. What is true for the individual is also true for the whole. And because of our place as microcosm, our individual consciousness can directly interact with the energy of the whole, and begin to release the hidden potential in its patterns of interrelationship. Our light can flow into the whole of life, just as it can go into our own depths, and begin the work of transformation.

It is important to remember that as life is a single living organism, our light is part of the light of the whole. Life is using us, using our light in order to wake up. It is drawing us into this drama of global awakening. And the first step is to return the light of the individual to the whole of creation. The previous era's drama of separation has resulted in an image of ourselves as separate from life, of individual life as separate from the life of the whole. Spiritual disciplines were also drawn into this dynamic, creating an image of an inner journey separate from the outer world. In order to regenerate itself, the whole now needs the spiritual light of those who have committed themselves in service to the whole. And those whose light has been even partly freed from the constrictions of form, have an energy and a freedom that allow them to work within the energy structure of life in a way that is inaccessible to those who remain caught in life's images.

At the beginning of our own journey we need to be reminded of our own higher purpose. Through spiritual practices or the presence of a teacher, the energy of the Self, which is our higher consciousness, is released to enable the inner work to happen. Without this impulse of energy we could not make the shift out of our previous patterns and the grip of the ego. The world too needs an impulse of energy to make its shift into the next era; it also needs to be reminded of its higher purpose, its divine nature. Those who look towards God, who uncompromisingly live their divine nature, can help in this work of remembrance. Through the remembrance of their own heart, a light can be given to the world to help it to remember.

Through the higher consciousness of the individual, the work of awakening the world and reminding it of its true purpose can begin. Previously such spiritual work was done only by spiritual masters, by those who looked after the spiritual well-being of the world. But a hallmark of the new era is that this work is given back to humanity, to those who are awake enough to participate in it. It is no longer hidden or secret; it is being given into our collective consciousness. At present only a few are awake enough to recognize this, and many sincere spiritual seekers are too involved with their own image of spiritual progress to step into this global arena. But the work is beginning. The first steps have already been taken. Spiritual groups and certain individuals have been positioned in the inner and outer worlds where they are needed, and certain connections between groups and individuals have been made. The next step is to begin to bring a higher light of divine consciousness into the world where it is needed, into the global patterns of interrelationships that are being created. Then the light of divine service will begin to flow around the world, and the world can begin to remember its true purpose.

THE LIFE-GIVING POWER OF IMAGES

The importance of these images, the world-wide web, for example, or the individual as microcosm, is that they provide a connection between the inner and outer worlds. Traditionally symbols are seen as an intermediary between the visible world and the world of the soul—it is interesting that the Internet has given us a world of cyberspace that does not belong completely to the physical world but is its own virtual reality. As mediators of outer and inner, giving outer symbolic form to inner processes, these images enable us to participate consciously in what is happening inwardly—they align our consciousness with life's inner unfolding. The importance of conscious participation cannot be overstated. As the discoveries of particle physics are making us aware, consciousness plays a more active and determining role in the formation of matter than the detached observer of Newtonian physics could have imagined. An understanding of the dynamic interrelationship among matter, energy, and consciousness, understood by some of the alchemists, is now emerging in our science. We do not yet know what this might mean in our everyday life beyond making us aware that our consciousness is an actively determining part of life. But the image of consciousness that this points to is itself something new to our collective understanding, outside the range of the images that dominated the previous era. It is not a consciousness that controls life from outside, imposing itself through science and technology; it is part of the very creation of matter, the way life manifests into form.

Through dreams, visions, or synchronicities, our inner self gives us images and symbols that can help to align us with our own individual inner changes. At the level of the macrocosm, life itself is also giving us images, along with those that come from our inner self, to attune our conscious and unconscious self with the real changes that are taking place within the body of the world. As our consciousness recognizes these images, it adds its divine spark to the patterns that are unfolding. This spark can help the image come fully alive and realize its potential. Through our conscious recognition we bring the image into being, bring it from the inner world into the web of life where it can start to transform life itself.

Our initial work is to notice such images amidst the myriad distractions of our culture, and to begin to work with them. The images that belong to life's unfolding have a numinosity and vibrancy quite distinct from the dead images of our consumer culture. They are life speaking to us in its most ancient language, communicating with our soul, not our ego. They bring hope rather than empty promises. And they empower us rather than making us feel victims of a disconnected world. They are calling us to relate to life in a new way, no longer focused on our self-interest, material or spiritual. They have a quality of oneness and bring an ancient memory of another time, when humanity and the earth were in harmony and the earth and all of life were sacred, before the world was torn apart by power and greed. They remind us of something essential within us: that we are all a part of the same earth and carry the same divine purpose. These images are the soul of the world speaking to us, reminding us of what is real.

In every era the divine imprint within life comes alive in a new way. At the beginning there are only a few who notice this, who are not caught in the images of the past and so can recognize something new. But at the beginning all that is needed are a few to welcome in what is being born. This is how it has always been. What is different in this era is that it is no longer a secret to be protected, not a hidden mystical truth that needs the esoteric knowledge of the *magi*, the initiated few who can recognize and follow the new star. What is being born is all around us because this is a global awakening. And it is something very simple and ordinary, a quality of joy, a recognition that we are one.

COUNTERING THE FORCES OF DARKNESS

But there are real obstacles. There are powerful forces within our collective that would manipulate these images for their own ends. They do not want humanity as a whole to be given access to sources of power and energy that would usurp their control and dominance. These forces are outwardly visible in global corporations; they have spread their tentacles into many aspects of our life, including our imagination. We sense how pervasive they have become in exploiting our hopes and dreams, steering our desires and even our life energy in directions they deem profitable. But we do not fully realize how these forces exist in the inner world as well, manipulating the images of our psyche, leeching the natural joy out of life. Just as we are surrounded by outer ecological devastation, so do we also inhabit an inner wasteland where once there was beauty and numinosity, in which the images that would nourish the soul have been polluted by the forces of consumerism.

These negative forces are trying to stop new, life-giving images from coming into our collective consciousness. Therefore it is not enough just to recognize the new images. They need to be given energy to sustain them—they need to be empowered. Otherwise they will be repressed or manipulated, just as the image of globalization has become a tool for a more complete corporate exploitation. One cannot avoid these negative forces—they are continually around us in the "McDonaldization" of our world. To fight against them is rarely effective; they have become too pervasive, too much part of our economic structure and daily life. What we can do effectively is to give power to the new life-sustaining images that are being born. It is these images that can recreate inner and outer life amidst our present wasteland. In the words of Carl Jung, "The archetypal images decide the fate of man."[3]

How can one give enough energy to these emerging images to counter the forces of materialism? Working in isolation, one could never give them enough energy. But it is the organic nature of life to create a web of light and consciousness that can help this process. A network of light has already been formed in the inner worlds, created by the masters of love and their disciples in order to help humanity emerge into the next era. This network of light exists on the plane of pure being where it cannot be corrupted by the darkness of the world. It is directly connected to the source of life, where the pure energy of creation comes into being. This inner network is now being connected to a network of individuals and spiritual groups, sustaining them from within, giving them access to energy that would otherwise be veiled from them. Through this outer network, this organic linking of individuals, energy can flow from the inner worlds to individual consciousness and so empower the images that are needed to recreate our world. It is a simple process through which the light-cells of life that are within human consciousness are being realigned so that life on all levels can be recreated in a self-sustaining way.

Sustained and nourished by the light of a network of consciousness, the images of life can come into existence according to their original intent, not distorted or controlled by the negative forces that at present dominate our collective. Through these images a new era can be born into our collective consciousness and thus into our world.

These are images based upon the organic wholeness of life and humanity's central role within this wholeness as a co-creator, part of the divine intelligence of which all of life is an expression.

Our light is part of the light of the world, and, as the alchemists understood, it has a unique role in realizing the true potential of matter. It is through our light that the light hidden in matter can be released. And when this light hidden within the world, the *lumen naturae*, is released, the true purpose of creation will once again become visible—"In Thy light shall we see light."[4] Life will awaken to its divine nature.

However, as a first step we must offer ourselves as midwife to the images that life is giving to us. This means being receptive to these images as they come to us from the inner and outer worlds, and recognizing their value. Through our individual consciousness they take on the divine light of the world, and when our consciousness is linked together with the consciousness of others, it has the power to sustain these images. We need to recognize the power of individual consciousness to sustain the images that can redefine our experience of the world. Humanity is being given the tools to transform the world, and yet we are reluctant to fully step into this arena. Perhaps we would prefer to remain children, blaming others, governments, corporations for all that is wrong in our world, refusing the responsibility our real power and light confer upon us—and in the process surrendering our power and light to the collective darkness. Real self-empowerment means accepting responsibility for this work that needs to be done.

5.

CHANGING THE DREAM

For each age is a dream that is dying,
Or one that is coming into birth.

Arthur O'Shaughnessy[1]

The shamans of Latin America teach us that we can
shape-shift our world: First you have a dream. Then
you make a commitment to the dream. You apply
energy to that dream and every day take action of
some sort to make that dream a reality. If you do
this you will make the dream happen. That's basically
what we've done in the U.S. over the past century.
We've created this very prosperous country where
we have lots of cars and lots of money to buy things.
Now we have to come up with a new dream.

John Perkins[2]

We see around us a dream that is dying. Any species
that destroys its own ecosystem is moving towards self-
extinction. There is also a dream that is being born, a
dream of global oneness and interconnectivity which
reflects the divine unity of creation. This dream demands
our attention in order to come into being. The images
of life's oneness and interconnectivity are calling for us
to work with them, to engage in the timeless alchemical
work of transmutation in which we take real responsibility
for what is being born. We are the crucible in which the
everyday and the sacred are being reunited. Through us a

way of life is being born into consciousness that connects everything together according to its essential nature. We do not fully recognize or value this process in which we play such a central role; it appears so ordinary that we overlook it. But it is here, in ourselves, in our everyday life, in the patterns of connections through which we relate to the world, that the real changes are waiting to happen, and where we can begin the work of transmuting the dream that is becoming so destructive to our present world.

RECLAIMING THE CONNECTION
BETWEEN THE INNER AND OUTER

The dream that presently dominates our collective consciousness is born from our delight in materialism, our infatuation with what we can buy to improve our lives. Clothes, electronics, new cars—these images saturate our airwaves and thought-forms. If we only look, we can see that they do not sustain us, that in fact they draw energy from us—they take not just from our bank accounts but also from our life force. Turning away from the gods of old that used to sustain life, we have created our own new ones—insatiable gods of materialism that make us work harder and harder to placate them. How many hours a week do we work to pay for our pleasures, the material indulgences we think are necessary for life?

We may have dismissed the archetypal world, but the archetypal world is still with us; it has only taken on another form and become more demonic. When we reject a conscious relationship with the archetypes, they enter through the shadow, through our weaknesses and desires. Here they absorb us and drain our energy and attention, or turn our energy negative so that we attack others to feed them. We may justify America's drive for global and political dominance as "protecting our way of life," but how much of what propels that way of life is our need to feed this monster of acquisition and consumption we have created?

And might there also be a darker reason for the poverty of our present images? Could it be that the forces of that sacred dimension which we no longer respect and whose images we have excluded from our world still retain their power, and that they are not happy in their neglect? Our rejection and suppression of the feminine, our mistreatment of the earth, have pushed the power of the goddess into the shadows, where energy so easily turns destructive—and she has turned her spells against us, entrapping us in her material world without access to the images that would open us to matter's sacred, transformative dimension. Our traditional fairy tales vividly remind us of the danger of rejecting the dark feminine, but one need only look at what the expression "fairy tales" has come to mean in our culture to see how we have dismissed the wisdom they contain. Cut off from any living images of the forces we have banished, we remain firmly imprisoned in our greed, caught by images of material prosperity, not realizing their dark secret: there is an aspect of the Great Mother that devours and destroys even her own children. Could it be that from deep in the shadows of our neglect she is still exerting her power, entangling us in her veils, enthralling us with her seductive play of images, yet cutting us off from her nourishment—exacting her revenge?

We can see the emptiness of today's images as caused by a culture that has consciously divorced itself from the sacred, focusing on material prosperity and starving the soul. Or we could see it as the Great Mother enacting her revenge against those who have denied her. Materialism has become a force of the dark mother, "mater," entrapping us more and more in her destructive web.

We are very unconscious of the forces that dominate and drive us. We see only the surface of things. But if we are to change the present dynamics of global exploitation and imbalance our "way of life" has created—if we are to change this dream that is strangling us—we will have to look beneath the surface to the forces that have created them, and these are not just socio-economic or ecological. In the archetypal world, much more powerful forces control us. Only if we turn back to this inner realm and change the dynamics of these archetypal forces do we have any chance to create a global culture that can sustain itself into the future—to create the dream that will shape the next era.

In previous cultures the way to change a negative relationship with the unconscious was for a shaman or healer to journey inward and confront or communicate with the negative energy. The shaman knew the ways of the inner world; he knew how to travel there and invoke beneficial and helpful forces, as well as how to counter the negative forces that can be so destructive. He knew how to retrieve a soul that had gotten lost, which is what happens when a central part of ourself gets caught in the unconscious. Assisted by his culture's rituals, chanting, sacred dance or music, he could help the individual or the tribe to integrate the inner and outer life.

In our present culture we have become caught in our unconscious materialistic drives, feeding our archetypal monsters with the resources of our planet as well as our life energy, upsetting the delicate balance of our planetary ecosystem as well as of our own soul. And we have lost the understanding of how to counter this imbalance. We urgently need to reclaim this knowledge; we need to heal the soul of the world, to evoke the inner powers that are necessary if we are to confront the real forces of materialism—not the marketing strategies of our corporations, but the inner demons that are pushing us into this self-destructive and soul-denying cycle of greed. The dark energies that have gripped our collective consciousness are very real, and they need our attention.

How can we reclaim the knowledge of working with the inner world and adapt it to the needs of the present time—to the global dimension of the danger that is threatening us? The traditional way of the shaman, with its magical techniques, its secrets often passed down through the generations according to closely guarded traditions, its demanding initiations, belongs mainly to the past.[3] But in each era this knowledge is given anew, according to the needs of the time and the future that is being born—this is part of the esoteric mystery of life, how it midwifes its own rebirth as the sacred takes on a new form, communicates in a new language. Today, we will find what is needed not in any hidden esoteric tradition, but in life itself—in the world around us and in ourselves. It is here, in our lives, within us, all around us, that we will find the doorway to the inner realms. And if we can learn to be present there, at the place in ourselves and in life where the inner and outer worlds meet, where the forms of life are coming into being, we will have access to the knowledge we need.

How can we access this place where the worlds meet, where the inner comes into form? The real question to ask is why we exclude ourselves from this place. Why do we live at the very periphery of ourselves where only the outer world has meaning? The inner world is not hidden in secret places but is all around us and within us. Its magic may be muted in our contemporary lives, its power overlooked, but it is still present, in our dreams and nightmares, our hopes and fears, and we can no longer deny them. Nor can we any longer reject the ancient trust that has been placed in us as guardians of the planet—and not just of her physical form but also her soul.

If we go within ourselves, we will find that there is a simple connection between us and the source of life, a way of being that is part of our very nature in which our spiritual and natural selves align themselves in harmony and nourish each other. It is in our breath, and if we live consciously, it is present in every step we take. This connection is the place in us where the worlds meet. It can be veiled by the forms of our self-created world; when we live an artificial life, we lose our awareness of it, and then we live divorced from our natural self and life as it really is. But when we recognize the divine in ordinary life, when we practice the simple awareness of breath throughout our day, we return to our real condition, to this natural connection we embody. The soul celebrates its presence in the two worlds: in the outer world of the senses and the inner world which is its home. Holding the consciousness of this connection, we live where the two worlds meet and can work to bring our planet back into balance.

It is not necessary to search for shamans in the remote rainforest or deserts to discover the secrets we need. The era of global oneness awakens us to a knowing that is present everywhere. We are the knowing. Our connection to life and to the inner world is the connection we need. Life has its own healing center, which is within each of us. When we remain isolated within our separate self, this center is dormant. But once we acknowledge that we are an integral part of the living organism of the earth and are willing to participate in its rebirth, this healing potential can be directly activated.

We need to be consciously connected to the inner and outer worlds, and to be fully present. Only then can we access the power and knowledge within us that is life itself, life that is the song of the soul and not just a succession of desires and fantasies.

THE CONNECTIONS OF LIFE

Within each of us lies the knowledge of how the worlds work together, how the images of the soul come into being and determine the fate of humanity. This knowing is a part of life, part of the miracle of creation. When we are present both within ourselves and in our life, we can see the patterns of connection that bring things together— the ordinary human connections of our outer life, between family, friends, and colleagues; connections of trade and commerce that move goods, services, and money through our local and global marketplace; and now all the new connections created by global communication, by the Internet, satellite TV, and cell phones. We are also beginning to rediscover the interconnections of our ecosystem that knit all of creation together into a single living organism, and if we pay attention we can begin to rediscover the deeper connections between the inner and outer worlds that bring the meaning of the soul into our daily life. And underlying everything are the connections of pure love that link together all of creation with the Creator. We live in the midst of so many connections, and there is so much power and meaning in these connections that we presently overlook.

The connections of life are its lifeblood. We are physically nourished by our natural ecosystem, and also by the connections of trade that bring food to our tables. We are emotionally nourished by our family and friends, and sustained in emotional and practical ways by the different types of communication that play an increasingly important part in our life, the cell phone and e-mail that have so quickly become a vital source of connection. The connections of the soul are more hidden in our culture, but are present in our dreams and in our search for meaning. And the primal connection of love that is the foundation of creation is what nourishes us all at the deepest level—and, paradoxically, what we all search for, knowingly or unknowingly.

We are at the center of so many connections, and yet we imagine ourselves isolated and alone. Our isolation is one of the most potent myths of our time, and it keeps us from consciously receiving the nourishment that comes through these different levels of connection. We feel disempowered because we feel alone, rather than being supported and empowered by the whole of which we are an integral part. Even as we are being given conscious access to a greater degree of connectivity than ever before, our entrapment in our myth of aloneness makes us feel more and more separate. Stepping into a global era still caught in the conditioning of the previous era, we remain cut off from and unaware of the real potential of what we are being offered.

Life is recreating itself through these patterns of connection and the relationships they form. This is the primal oneness of life expressing itself in new ways. Yet this simple awareness that life is one seems too threatening to fully accept. Seeing our interconnectedness through the veils of separation, we fear that it might take something away from us. We easily withdraw into old patterns of protection, defending our autonomy, our possessions, our status, and are thus unable or unwilling to embody its real meaning. But all these patterns of connection are just ways through which the oneness of life is manifesting itself, and the more we are aware of this, the more we can embody the power and dynamism that belong to life's oneness. Unity is far more powerful than separation.

As a part of life's oneness, we can never be isolated. When we pick up the phone or connect to the Internet, we *know* that we are part of a global network of communication that is instantaneously available. We wear clothes that are made in distant countries, and when we change the channels on our TV we see images from across the globe. Even the food we eat now comes from all over the world, making us part of life's ecosystem as well as the network of trade that brought it to our table. We are all a part of this interrelated oneness, and yet we have not fully grasped the real opportunity this is offering us. It is as if we were watching a movie frame by frame, never seeing the connection between the frames and so never getting the story the movie is telling. And the story we are missing is our own story, the meaning of our own life seen through the eyes of oneness.

THE LANGUAGE OF ONENESS

Life is speaking to us in the language of oneness. We persist in trying to read it with our old vocabulary of separation and we are missing what it is telling us. Still caught in our conditioned ideas of separateness, still asking what life can give to us (or what we can get from life), we cannot decipher life's message of its deep interrelatedness, nor can we see how this reflects life's real nature as a living organism. It is very difficult for life to communicate with someone who is seeing himself as separate from the whole. This is one of the reasons we seem so impotent at this time of global crisis. We are looking at the book of life without recognizing its language—or more disastrously, mistranslating it into a language of our own invention, a language that has nothing to do with the story that is unfolding now in the world.

When we step out of the self-imposed prison of our own isolation, life can start to tell us its story of oneness and interconnectivity, and it can show us how to live it. Rather than imposing our beliefs or values on life, we need to learn to listen and to watch. Then we can discover what the Creator and the creation are communicating to us. Life can show us how to be present in the world in a way that respects and benefits all of creation. Our inner and our outer life can show us how the inner and outer worlds work together so that the meaning of the soul comes into our life. The signs are all around us; we just need to learn how to read them. The first step is to recognize that we have made the transition into an era of oneness and these signs are written in the language of oneness. Without this simple awareness we will go on stumbling in the dark—and our present darkness is only growing darker. The dream we have been living is becoming a nightmare.

The language of life is our language. The oneness it expresses is an essential part of who we are. We have simply forgotten it, just as we have forgotten the ancient symbolic language of our dreams. There are many of life's languages we have forgotten: the language of plants and herbs that revealed the wisdom and secrets of healing, the language of the land and the weather that told earlier farmers when to plant and when to harvest, the language of the ocean which spoke to sailors of the ways of the sea.[4] All these languages, and the knowledge and wisdom they contain, express the oneness of life. But even though we have forgotten, we still carry that knowing within us, it is in our genes. Now, through the tools of global communication, it is coming back into our consciousness in a new vocabulary; life is reawakening it, reflecting it to us anew.

If we can let go of our old language and myths and mental habits of separation, we can enter into the paradigm of oneness that is beginning to emerge. We can read the signs that are becoming visible in life and within ourselves. We can learn how life is being born anew at this time and *we can participate in its rebirth*. We can align our consciousness with the wholeness of life on both an organic and symbolic level and come to know the part we have to play in its unfolding.

RECOGNIZING LIFE'S NEW SYMBOLS

In the symbolic depths within ourselves and within the world, new patterns are forming, new ways for life to come into being. These will constellate into the images and symbols that will help shape the coming era. Our job is to recognize them, and to help them be born into the world. In order to do this, we need to be present between the worlds, at the symbolic core of ourselves where life comes into form.

The symbolic world lies at the very threshold of consciousness, present and yet not fully acknowledged. When we make a conscious connection with the images that arise from the symbolic world, we gain access to its real power, its deeply transformative potential. The symbolic world belongs to the soul, and when we acknowledge this sacred dimension, it can open and communicate to us in a way that is unimaginable in the dream which is dying, which has denied us access to these depths.

Symbols act as a bridge between the inner and the outer worlds, allowing the energy and meaning of the inner to flow into the outer. They can bring into life primal energies that have not been polluted or conditioned, which we can then creatively channel. The images of oneness that are emerging into our consciousness are life itself drawing us back to its source, back to the pure waters of life that flow from its essence.[5] The water from the source has a healing quality; whatever it touches is purified and reconnected to its essential nature. And it has a quality of joy that belongs to life's essential nature—a quality that is sadly missing in our contemporary culture.

If we open to the symbolic dimension of these images, they can connect us directly to the source of life, to the energies at work in creation. At the beginning of a new era, a direct connection can be made with the new energy of creation that comes from the Source. When a culture has developed, that energy, though it is still present, becomes less accessible, covered over by the cultural and religious developments of the era. But at the beginning it is possible to have access to the freedom and vitality that are an expression of life's regeneration; to be present where life comes into being.

But we are so immersed in the many distractions of today's culture that we do not notice the symbolic dimension of the new images that life is giving us, and so we are unaware of their primal power. Living on the surface of our lives, we are not present in the place between the worlds where we can access their symbolic dimension, which is the source of their real potential. When we think of the Internet, for example, we see only a tool for communication or commerce. We do not see that it is a living expression of a new consciousness that has within it access to energies and powers that can completely rearrange our world. If we were awake to its real symbolic potential, we would be truly in awe—and we would laugh, with wonder, at life's capacity to recreate itself while we are not even looking.

The Internet is a powerful, living image of life's oneness. As it becomes more and more present in our collective consciousness, it is more and more able to channel life's underlying energies in new ways. It is a power and life force of its own, able to evolve and adapt like a fast-changing organism, and, like other emerging images of our time, it is reconfiguring our consciousness, helping us to interact with life in new ways.

Like all symbols, the Internet will reveal the secret of its real potential only if we approach it with the right attitude and acknowledge its sacred dimension. At the same time, working with these emerging images requires a different attitude from the one we bring to symbols that relate only to the inner—or spiritual—dimension. In our Western culture we tend to see symbols as separate from everyday life, usually relegating them to sacred or religious ceremonies. It is many centuries since we have related to the ordinary activities of our daily life as having a symbolic dimension. And what could be more "mundane," more of our everyday world, than the Internet? To access the symbolic within the mundane requires that we lose that "spiritual" conditioning and free ourselves from its restrictions.

Yes, it can be a shock to recognize that the sacred is revealing itself in something as mundane as the technology of the Internet or cell phone communication. But we need to be aware that the divine reveals itself in the most unexpected ways. Often, like Khidr, the Sufi figure of direct revelation, the divine appears as something so ordinary we do not recognize it until afterwards, and so miss the real opportunity of the meeting. We need to be alert, to realize that the symbols that will shape the dream of the next era are likely to turn up in the places we least expect them—in ourselves, in the ordinariness of our daily lives.[6] Then we can open ourselves to the laughter and joy in the way the divine awakens us to a new way of being, turning our "spiritual" perception upside down once again!

CO-CREATING WITH THE SYMBOLIC WORLD

When we relate to a symbol and acknowledge its spiritual dimension, it can communicate directly with our soul. Symbols can take us into a dimension of ourselves that embraces all of this life and the beyond. They are a living expression of a reality that permeates the physical world and yet is not caught in its limitations. They give us access to our own divine nature and the divine within all of life.

Once we understand how these images arise from within life, we will give them the correct attention, and start a creative dialogue with the symbolic world. This is part of the co-creative relationship that humanity is being offered, in which the individual can interact directly with the whole. As we help bring into being the symbols that can heal and nourish the soul of the world, we begin to live this responsibility. We take on our role as guardians of the planet, and we do so with the consciousness of oneness that includes and connects the sacred and the mundane, the inner and the outer, spirit and matter, the world's soul and body and our own, the individual and the planet.

The relationship between the individual soul and the soul of the world is partly a symbolic communion in which we help create and bring into consciousness the images that can nourish us on all levels. The relationship between the soul and the physical world can be more beneficial than we realize: through it the outer world can be nourished by the energies and powers of the soul. In previous ages this work helped the crops to grow and kept the people spiritually sustained. Today we need it to heal the world. Working with this relationship, we can retrieve the part of the soul of the world that has been lost, and help reconnect our outer world to its "power animals," the archetypes that can help the world continue its journey. There is much work to be done between the worlds, connecting together the inner and outer, and rediscovering the sources of power that we need in order to evolve as a whole. And with this work can be born the science of the future that gives us an understanding of how the inner and outer work together: how the energies of the inner worlds can nourish our outer life, and how our outer life can nourish our soul.

Oneness means bringing these worlds back into harmony, learning how they communicate with each other and work together as part of a greater whole. The past era of separation has divided the worlds, and now we have to heal this divide. Symbols are being born in both worlds to facilitate this reunion of inner and outer, but they need our conscious attention. They need our spark of consciousness to come fully alive and begin the real work of global transformation.

And at the same time we will have to face our reluctance to step fully into the dimension of the soul and acknowledge our responsibility. We will have to face our shame at how we have treated this sacred dimension of ourselves and our planet, and our fear of what we will find in the inner world—the monsters we have created through our neglect and denial of the sacred. The terrorists who have forced their way into our collective consciousness could be an expression of a deeper darkness we will have to face in the inner world. It is always easier to blame someone else than confront the darkness.

There are many reasons we might prefer not to take on our responsibility, but there is work to be done with the symbolic consciousness of the world. And this work can only be done on an individual level—it is through the relationship between the individual and the symbolic world that healing and transformation can come. Alchemically it is the spark of individual consciousness, crossing into the inner world, that is the catalyst for transformation. Communion with the sacred is always an individual act. This is part of the mystery of the soul's relationship to the world and to God.

Working with the symbolic world has always been a part of our human heritage. We need to reawaken to this ancient heritage and use it to harmonize our outer life with the inner forces of creation—to create a civilization that can use the resources of both worlds in a way that is creative and nourishing for all of life and for the soul of humanity. What makes this time different from previous eras is that now the individual is needed to participate in co-creating the symbolic structure of the world, which will shape the ways the primal energy within creation expresses itself in life, and so the individual is being given more direct access to the soul of the world than ever before.

INDIVIDUAL RESPONSIBILITY
AND THE ARCHETYPAL WORLD

Any time of transition has unexpected dangers. This is especially true of this time of transition in our relationship with the symbolic world. Carl Jung wrote that the symbols of the unconscious place a great responsibility upon the individual.[7] If a symbol arises from the unconscious and is not consciously related to, it can turn inward and become devouring rather than creative. This is the negative side of an archetype, imaged in the *ouroboros*, the serpent eating its tail. In the primal depths of the unconscious, nothing is born; the energy feeds back into itself. Our only protection from this devouring aspect of the inner world is consciousness. The reflective stance of consciousness acts as a mediating mirror, like Perseus' shield,[8] enabling us to work with the unconscious without being overwhelmed or paralyzed by its raw power. Without this mediating quality of consciousness, the psyche devours, or turns to stone, everything it encounters.

Symbols arise from the unconscious, whose natural power easily pulls us into its depths. Just as there are forces of evolution that push us towards consciousness, there are balancing forces that draw us back into unconsciousness, and archetypes and symbols constellate this power. At times of transition in our relationship to the symbolic world, both forces will come into play on a collective level. When a symbol or archetype begins to appear, it has a raw power that is unconstrained by the behavioral patterns of a culture that condition our behavior and help keep it within civilized bounds—and it can easily pull an individual, a group, or a society into its grip. As we saw in Bosnia and Rwanda, and are now seeing in Iraq, where the raw power of tribal identity turns neighbors into murderers, torturers, or rapists, an archetypal energy can overwhelm the patterns of behavior and morality of our religious and cultural conditioning that defend us psychically against these amoral energies of the unconscious. Earlier in the last century Jung witnessed the same pattern, as the German people were collectively swept up by the archetype of the warrior god Wotan; even before the outbreak of the First World War he had seen the rivers of blood that subjugation to such an archetype would demand.

Cultural conditioning protects us, but it also limits our growth. At times of transition the protective conditioning needs to break down so that something new can be born. Our conscious attention is needed at such times, to act as a balance against the primal pull of the unconscious as the new symbol or archetype arises. Without our consciousness, the raw power of the archetype can draw us into the depths from which it emerged, where it can feed negative energies. We see this happening now all around us: rather than global union we are experiencing a global religious fanaticism as well as a resurgence of violent tribalism. How much of our energy is being drawn into these dark vortexes? And with our present Western values that are self-centered and divisive rather than unifying, we are impotent to stop this hemorrhaging of our life force, unable to stop feeding the destructive, insatiable gods that have taken hold in our unconscious.

A relationship with the gods is demanding and difficult. It is all too easy to slip into unconsciousness, seduced by their power, and become their victims. Only individual consciousness can counter the pull of the unconscious. This is not a work that any religion, organization, or government can do. It is the individual hero who traditionally defeats the monster, symbolizing the role of our individual consciousness in this archetypal drama. This is the responsibility of each one of us.

The gift of free will banished us from the innocence of the Garden of Eden and gave us the responsibility for our own destiny. Paradoxically, this dawning global era is giving more responsibility to the individual than ever before. Still caught in our old images of isolation and separation, we have not yet grasped that the meaning of this responsibility lies in the relationship of the microcosm and macrocosm, the individual and the whole, nor do we recognize the power and potential for real change that this relationship gives to us.

Every era has its dream. At this time when an old era is dying and a new one being born, it is up to each of us to take conscious responsibility for the images of oneness that are now emerging from the symbolic depths. These images will shape the dream of the new era. Our participation will determine how these images come into being and whether they will take us out of the current nightmare of greed and separatist fanaticism that is destroying our planet and causing such suffering to so many, and into a new way of living with the earth. They can give us hope, a vision of wholeness, and sustain us with the energy and meaning we need to co-create a new world.

6.

THE ALCHEMY OF THE ARCHETYPAL WORLD

The archetypes are the great decisive factors,
they bring about the real events....
The archetypes decide
the fate of man.

C. G. Jung

WALKING IN BOTH WORLDS

Every step we make, like every breath we take, is a meeting of the inner and outer worlds. We may not consciously know it, but at every moment we are alive in both worlds. The inner is the ground from which our soul draws its sustenance, not in some abstract sense, but in a very real way. We could not live if we did not walk continually in the inner. We have been conditioned to believe that we live only in the world we perceive through our senses, but a simple recognition of how our fantasies, fears, and imaginings influence us reveals that we also inhabit a less tangible world. Animals may live only in the outer, physical world. We do not. We are driven by desires and demons, longings and fears, most of which have their origin in the inner world rather than our outer reality. We are creatures of our own psyche and the vaster maze of the collective unconscious, nourished as much by our dreams and fears as we are by food and water.

We breathe the air of both worlds. Sometimes a hidden fragrance from the inner world can catch our attention and lead us down unexpected avenues, around corners we never thought to turn, giving us a brief glimpse of life's inner dimension. The pestilence of the inner world can also affect us, though we rarely recognize the ways its darkness draws us—we walk for the most part as if the tangible ground were all we tread upon, as if the emissions of our automobiles and our industries were the only bad air we breathe.

It is true that since the advent of psychology we have to some degree come to recognize the inner world of our own personal psyche. We have realized that there may be disturbances that come from within; we are allowed to have personal phobias. But this image of the inner does not begin to encompass the larger world of the collective unconscious we also live in, the swirling, immaterial world of our collective hopes and fears. We do not acknowledge our collective dreaming, and we do not consider how much our outer actions are driven or determined by these forces of the inner world.

Soon we will have to wake up, to accept the reality of both worlds. We cannot afford to pretend much longer: our collective fears are becoming too dark, our material fantasies unsustainable. We will have to accept that the inner worlds were never really banished by the Age of Reason, and that we are still frightened of their darkness, just as we are seduced by their siren-like temptations. We may have to consider how much we are depleting our personal and collective resources by ineffectually fighting these unseen monsters, by trying to protect ourselves from these fears. Can all of our security measures help us when the real threat is an inner demon? Similarly, can all our striving really fulfill our dreams, when the source of our desires is an ethereal temptress or the longing of the soul?

Life is a mystery and not a problem. It is a mysterious coming together of the worlds, a continual breathing in and out in which the physical and the dream worlds interpenetrate within us. Walking in both worlds, we are the place where the worlds meet, where the insubstantial takes on form and the physical reveals its foundation in the symbolic. We have both a symbolic and a physical existence, and only when we understand their relationship can we live a grounded and meaningful life. We may have been told that to be grounded means to be fully present in the physical everyday world, but this is only another myth, more propaganda. It is the symbolic that underlies the physical, as every earlier culture understood. The symbolic gives both substance and meaning to the physical; it is our real grounding.

Part of our difficulty in understanding this is that all of our collective power structures and ideologies acknowledge only the outer world. In the West, the Catholic Church decided early on that temporal power was more important than the world of the spirit, and it used the torture of the Inquisition to finally stamp out any real relationship to inner dimensions. And now in our current culture, though there may be individuals who have made their own relationship with the inner, there remain no shamans or priests to help us collectively. We are stranded on the shore of the material, scientific world we have created, without vessels or navigators to help us in the seas that are all around us. We can sense the power of these seas, feel the pull of their tides, their effect on our lives, but we do not know how to harness their energy, how to work with their primal forces.

Can we relearn collectively what we have forgotten? Can our present power structures acknowledge the real forces that influence our lives? At present those power structures try to manipulate our fears and desires, not realizing they are only tempting dragons they cannot control. The real forces underlying our fear of terrorism or our desire for material security are more powerful than our politicians imagine. And these forces cannot be stopped with bombs or prisons. They cannot be placated with cheap goods or new technologies. In myths such monsters demanded sacrificial virgins. Who is unknowingly being sacrificed today? Who are the virgins we have delivered to be devoured?

We cannot look to the collective for answers. The collective cannot right this imbalance, redeem this arrogance and ignorance; it cannot make a relationship with the inner world and its inhabitants. That work is up to individuals—we have to look to ourselves. Only as individuals can we make the connections needed to create a bridge that will link us once again with the world of the gods. It used to be the individual hero who fought the dragon and rescued the virgin. As a hero, he was an individual representing the collective, and the collective valued and honored its heroes. But today's collective does not acknowledge those who venture into the inner world of dragons. Our corporate culture does not even know they exist. Our corporations, so busy polluting the planet in the name of higher profits, could in fact be a manifestation of the monsters that devour our virgins.

At some point there will need to be a collective recognition of the inner world and its effect on our lives. But how can the collective recognize what it has been told for centuries does not exist? It might seem unrealistic to imagine that just a few individuals could redeem this blindness. But could it be that by building a bridge to the inner world they are creating a way for the archetypes themselves to effect this transformation, for the gods to awaken humanity to their existence? We are conditioned to believe things happen only through our own effort and striving; we have forgotten these forces have a wisdom and power far beyond our own.

Anyone who has really encountered these inner energies knows how powerful they are. These are the forces that shape civilizations. (Even materialism, that force that has so powerfully shaped Western life over the last centuries, is a goddess, a dark side of the Great Mother.) What matters is our relationship with them. When we deny them they can devour us. When we accept and respect them we can interact with them in a beneficial and creative relationship. Our consciousness is the key, and through the work of our individual consciousness we can create a relationship that welcomes them back into the world. We can open the door that we boarded up in our long collective embrace of rationalism. Once the archetypes are welcomed into the world of human consciousness, then they can do their work of making their presence felt. They have the power and wisdom to speak to the collective in a way that will be recognized. They will help the whole of humanity remember the inner world.

CONSCIOUSNESS AND THE GODS

When an individual ventures into the inner world and makes a conscious relationship with its archetypal energies, individual consciousness is the agent of transformation. It can change these forces from undifferentiated, amoral energies into forces that have a specific purpose and intention, and thus a creative effect. Our consciousness becomes their consciousness, our discrimination their discrimination. These powers lie beyond our ego-self and yet they are a part of us: they are part of the greater whole that is our real being. Thus our consciousness is also a part of them, and our focus and intention can become part of the way they express themselves.

The imagination is a vehicle for this relationship.[1]
Through active or creative imagination these primal
powers become visible in forms and images. Their vast
undifferentiated energy becomes more specific and thus
more accessible. The individual and also the collective
can then make a creative relationship with these forces
without being overwhelmed by their raw power, without
being sucked into unconsciousness.

We are beginning to understand how this works in the
context of traditional sacred art and some esoteric practices. The Tibetan monk who painted terrifying images of
the goddess was working not just with colors and symbols,
but with the dark energy of the sacred feminine. Through
these images both the artist and those who meditated
upon them could make a beneficial relationship with her
primal power. The detailed and specific techniques of an
icon painter have a similar purpose. Through meditating on
an icon of a saint, one could evoke the help of the divine
energy behind the figure. As with the gods and goddesses
of other traditions, the different saints imaged different
beneficial archetypal energies in the intermediate symbolic
world. Through prayers and meditations humanity used
these images to access and ask for help and healing from
the forces of the inner worlds. Some icons belonged to a
whole community, their energy and blessing considered a
vital part of communal life. Some, like the ancient shamanic
images of Tibetan deities, often painted on rocks, invoked
the primal forces that belonged to a specific place. These
images, working through art rather than sacrifice, helped
human beings both individually and collectively to create
a beneficial relationship with the inner world. The inner
world also taught some individuals how to be their mediums; shamans, healers, prophets, and some poets learned
how to be a mouthpiece of the inner world. The priestesses
at Delphi, for example, knew how to speak the voice of

the god, their messages, often paradoxical or enigmatic, expressing the ambiguous ways of the inner world.

Humanity's focus in working with these energies has always been on how they can help us. But at the same time that individuals or societies were making their relationship with these forces, the forces themselves were making a relationship with the world of consciousness. Any relationship is always two-way, always a dialogue. Through these images and spoken messages the deities were relating to humanity, finding a medium for expression in human consciousness. Through the work of the artist, the meditations of the monk, the utterances of its individual human mediums, the inner world was finding a way to communicate with the outer world, to tell it of its power or beauty, reveal the specific archetypal qualities of its different energies, relay its messages.

Without the medium of consciousness, the forces of the inner world still communicate, often through violent acts of nature or other disturbances that attract our attention (as on an individual level our unconscious may try to attract our attention through a physical symptom like a backache or some other psychological or physiological disturbance). Earlier societies understood these disturbances as communications from the inner world, often viewing natural disasters as a sign that they had displeased their gods, that they needed to attend to this relationship to put it back in balance. These primal powers of creation will do what they need to do to attract our consciousness. They do not themselves have consciousness, and they need our consciousness in order to express themselves: our consciousness is the bridge between the worlds, through which the inner can find expression in the outer.

The inner world needs to communicate and express itself in the outer world in order to change and evolve.

And we need to help that happen so that our outer world also can take the next step in its evolution. Inner and outer are dimensions of a single whole; they change and evolve together. If we can work from the perspective of the whole, seeing the oneness of life, we can begin to see that how we relate to the inner world of the archetypes is mirrored in how these primal energies of life relate to the outer world: if we consciously recognize them and treat them with respect, they in turn will be able to express themselves in the outer world in a creative and beneficial way. They will be allowed to serve life's highest purpose. If we do not, they may have to attract our attention by their ancient way of natural disasters. (From the evidence of the number and severity of recent major disasters, some might believe that has already begun to happen.) If the next stage of life's evolution is forced to occur in this way, life will still evolve, but it will happen much more slowly and painfully, and it will not be able to serve life's highest purpose in the same way.

In this evolution, consciousness is the key. This divine gift is our greatest contribution to life, to the inner and outer worlds. Through our consciousness the archetypal energies of the inner world gain a voice, a way to communicate and relate. At the present time they need to speak to humanity and communicate the necessity that we work together on an individual and on a collective level in this endeavor that belongs to both worlds, the work of reawakening the world.

HEALING THE ARCHETYPAL WORLD

Will we know how to listen when the gods speak to us? It has been so long since the gods spoke directly to humanity—only the gods of war still speak to us, in the language

of blood and destruction, and even there we have failed
to understand what they are telling us. But the changes in
the inner worlds could mean that a new way of relating is
also constellating for these forces. From the point of view
of our surface existence, the evolution of the inner worlds
seems more remote from what we take to be the realities
of our lives than a myth. But once we recognize that we
are all part of one whole, and that this wholeness includes
the inner as well as the outer world, then it is a simple step
to realize that as we evolve, these archetypal energies of
the inner world will evolve as well, and we will be able to
make a relationship with these inner changes.

In the inner world the patterns of change evolve
slowly over centuries. But these forces also experience
times of dramatic change, possibilities for a dramatic shift
in their evolution. This is such a time. And a crucial part
of this shift is the union of inner and outer. From a human
perspective this means an awareness that the inner and
outer are part of one whole and that we can no longer afford
to live the myth of separation. At this critical moment in
our evolution we have to reawaken to the reality of the
inner world and its archetypal inhabitants. We have to
relearn its symbolic language and live in creative harmony
with its forces. We have to give it an opportunity to work
directly with human consciousness, and through that
relationship to manifest and express itself in new ways.
Through human consciousness the evolution of the inner
world can be speeded up and new possibilities for growth
and change be constellated.

Our initial response might be, "What does this mean
for us?" But once we step back from our narrow focus on
ourselves and open to the greater vision that includes all
of creation, we can begin to think, "What might this mean
for these archetypal forces?" We care about the well-being
of living things, the plants and animals that inhabit our

natural world, for their own sake. It is just another step to include in that appreciation of life the living wholeness of inner and outer worlds, and to have concern for all of its inhabitants. We need to make this simple shift away from our self-interested concern towards a real appreciation and concern for the archetypal world for its own sake. We know in our own lives how the true concern of another person can help us to grow and flourish. The same is true for all of creation. Love, care, and attention are some of the greatest gifts we can give.

Real care and concern for the archetypal world will help to heal it from the damage our rejection and desecration have brought about. We have caused much pain in the archetypal world through our collective attitude. In particular, our treatment of the feminine, of the body of the world and its soul, has inflicted a grievous wound. It has created a veil of tears around the goddess, and spread a sense of isolation and desolation through the inner world. The world tree has forgotten the wonder of her fruits, their nourishing quality and their healing properties, and an inner wasteland has begun to take hold, creating dark and barren places of forgetfulness where before there were magical flowers of remembrance. A deep sorrow reigns in much of the inner world. Anyone who has journeyed there will have experienced the pain that is present; it has an endless quality that belongs to the timeless nature of the archetypal world. Something essential to life and existence is missing: the colors of creation that are formed in the inner world are losing their vibrancy, its pure and sparkling rivers are growing murkier, and some of its inhabitants have also forgotten their divine purpose. Our forgetfulness, our loss of connection with our soul, has affected the inner world, has gradually caused it too to forget. Our connection is their connection. The inner world cannot flourish without it. It needs our conscious remembrance.

As with all real work, our attitude is a powerful determining force. Our rejection of the inner has caused it much pain. Our love can help to heal it. Once an archetypal figure explained to me the importance of entering their world with the right attitude:

> Each time you come from your world to this inner world, and you come with love and understanding, not greed, then a grain of sand crosses the great divide. However small it may be, that grain of sand has immense meaning, for it comes with love. It forms part of an immense pattern like a mandala, and when this pattern is complete there will be a healing beyond all healing as the outer returns to the inner and the Self reveals itself. Then a new life will be upon your earth and upon my earth and there will be a flowering as there has not been for thousands of years.

If we come with the right attitude, the inner world will take us by the hand and instruct us how to redeem what we have polluted. The light of our consciousness can reawaken a light in the inner world, bring hope to places of despair. And our most precious gift to it is the fragrance of our divine remembrance, which helps the inner world to remember. The sweetness of our remembrance can help life's divine purpose to be reborn. And then the inner world can flower again; spring can come again to its inner wastelands—an unexpected spring that will catch us by surprise even if we have been waiting and longing for it. The inner world will wake up and its song will be heard, first in the inner and then in the outer world. The song of the inner world is the music of life and what is within life; it contains the purpose of creation and the wonder of being alive. And it comes from the depths of existence, from the forces that give birth to life. And once this song is heard again, the rivers of life will flow with joy in the inner worlds, and the beings of all the worlds will be nourished. And this is just the beginning.

AWAKENING TO THE SYMBOLIC WORLD

The forces of the inner world have been locked in the depths for centuries. Our dismissal and denial of their existence have become a prison for them. These primal powers of life have continued to direct us, through our instincts and other unconscious drives. But except through a few solitary individuals whose personal destiny has opened them to an inner communion, there has been very little direct communication with humanity, little conscious exchange. We have remained isolated in our surface world and the archetypes have withdrawn their voice. The soul of the world has become silent.

But now what has been kept separate is coming together: the veils between the worlds are being lifted. The world is awakening to its own oneness, and this includes the oneness of the different worlds. Inner and outer are coming together, and we cannot escape this, just as we cannot turn back the forces of globalization in the outer world. This coming together is a part of the greater destiny of the planet, a part of the planet's unfolding. The question is whether we can consciously work with it, rather than being drawn unwillingly and unconsciously into this new world that is being born.

The union of inner and outer can be a creative opportunity, an awakening to a hidden magic within life in which life's symbolic dimension comes alive. It has been so long since we have lived in a fully symbolic world that even our imaginations cannot yet take us there. When we experience the symbolic world as a living reality, when symbols come alive in our everyday existence, a whole new spectrum of life comes into consciousness. Everyday activities that have become meaningless and routine reveal themselves as part of life's mystery and draw us into its deeper purpose. Even now we can glimpse this, if, for example, when we connect to the Internet, we become aware of directly connecting to a web of life and consciousness around the planet, a web that is continually moving, changing, developing. In this instant we can experience our individual self as part of a dynamic whole, of patterns of relationship flowing across the world. The symbolic world is already present in our outer world. We just have to notice it—simply to look up for a moment from all our busyness, our self-importance, our thoughts and worries about the day, and look around us. Then we might see the vibrant colors of the dawn that is breaking.

What would it mean for the symbolic world to become fully alive? Our everyday life would lose its grayness and take on a new vibrancy. We would no longer need to satisfy an inner hunger with the accumulation of possessions, because we would be nourished directly from life, from its sacred substance that communicates through the symbolic. We would no longer need to search, often despairingly, for meaning, because meaning would be all around us. Life would open to us its book of meaning and on its pages we could more easily read the purpose of our individual existence. Life would speak to us directly about why we are here, and we could participate in life as it really is, in the joy of our real nature and purpose.

Of course there would still be difficulties and struggles, challenges, and the search for answers. But because life would be alive, it would be able to speak to us, reveal to us its sacred dimension. We would no longer have to make a deep and demanding inner journey to find meaning, because the inner and outer would have come together; the meaning would be *here*. This coming together is the *coniunctio* promised by the alchemists, the alchemical marriage from which a child is born. And this child is none other than our real self, a self that breathes with our every breath, that walks in this world with every step we take. The future that is being born *is* this child, a way to live our real self in everyday life. This is something so simple and so wonderful it is almost unimaginable.

When the world comes alive in this way we will no longer need artificial stimulants or all our present mechanisms of distraction. Life itself will nourish our body and our soul. We have lived for too long without this nourishment; we have grown pale and anemic as a result. Deprived of the sacred substance within life that is our real sustenance, we have struggled and fought to acquire a few crumbs from the table of life, a few temporary pleasures. But life is so much more than what we have asked of it: it is the divine becoming manifest, a wonder being revealed. The Garden of Eden from which we have been exiled is not heaven, but life. This is the world of divine presence into which we can be welcomed.

The symbolic world is the intermediary between the direct experience of the divine and the physical world of the senses. It allows the divine to come into our life without overwhelming us with its unlimited power. When the symbolic world is fully present in our everyday life, the divine will also be present, not in its overpowering force but in a way that we can digest. Its *manna* will be our daily bread.

Through the mediating power of symbols, we can reawaken to the mystery of life as a continual relationship with the divine, a constant communion. An opening to a real relationship with the divine within life is a gift of the sacred feminine—a gift that was ruthlessly rejected in the last era of masculine domination which banished the divine from creation, making it into something other than ourselves, other than life, to be attained only by turning away from life. That illusion will fall away when we once again open to life as a continual, moment-by-moment communion with the divine, when we realize that life in all its myriad forms is the divine speaking to us, and we are its response. Life is a dynamic interchange, an unceasing dialogue between the formless essence and the world of forms. All of creation is part of this dialogue, but only human consciousness can give it word and voice—can allow the divine to speak, and so make life conscious of its real nature and purpose, its essential divinity.

We are the consciousness of life, its voice in a divine dialogue. Within us the worlds come together and speak to each other, and the divine can speak within creation. This dialogue is central to the reawakening of life. Its energy is so dynamic that it can break up existing patterns of restriction within life and allow life to flow freely, to change and evolve according to its own divine principles. We think that the world follows only physical laws, but when the inner and the outer worlds come together again in dialogue, the divine will be able to express itself in life and a whole new set of principles will come into play. Divine oneness has its own laws, and they will free us of the isolation and constriction we have endured for so long.

THE SEDUCTIVE DARKNESS
OF THE ARCHETYPAL WORLD

The shadow side of this union of the worlds will manifest in the misuse of the powers of the inner world. We are familiar with the misuse of worldly power; we know its corruption and the suffering it creates, and we also know the strength of its temptation. As the inner door opens to powers that have been kept separate from life for centuries, there will be those who are drawn to misuse them, to engage in their dark magic, to turn the forces of creation to their own will. This is inevitable; free will always gives us choice. We can use our consciousness for the divine or for our own desires. It is the nature of life to allow us to choose the light or the dark or any of the variations and denials that lie between them, and some will be drawn into the darkness; they will use its magic in the world, creating fear and deceit where there might have been joy and a celebration of life.

We cannot avoid the dark forces, but we can learn to recognize them. We do not have to walk naively into the next age. We have traveled the roads of worldly power for too long not to have learned some wisdom and common sense. And of course we will each be tempted in our own way, offered ways to deceive ourselves and others. In our present world there are many forms of corruption, many colors of darkness, and the inner world will open us to more opportunity.

The archetypes themselves are amoral, which is why Jung stressed the importance of moral responsibility when encountering them. Their ambiguous nature can seduce and confuse us. When is the archetype of the warrior a hero and when is it a killer? When is the feminine arche-type of the prostitute sacred and when is it self-abusive? The clarity of our ordinary judgments cannot guide us in the archetypal realm. Sometimes the serpent is a bringer of wisdom from the depths, sometimes an image of a powerful life force we need, sometimes a symbol of a cold-blooded lack of feeling or care. The spider devours her children, allowing nothing new to develop or grow, and she also spins the web of creation, the patterns that sustain life.

Working with the inner world requires a much more acute discrimination than does our ordinary life. These forces are natural powers that care little for individual well-being; they are as indifferent to our private concerns as an earthquake or hurricane. Our image of an omniscient, caring divinity bears no resemblance to these inner gods and goddesses, who, the classical myths show, often behaved in cruel and unfeeling ways. They can be creatively channeled but not easily controlled. And as the ancient Greeks knew, they are not all celestial deities; some of these powers carry the dark, chthonic energies of the underworld. These archetypal forces can draw us easily into their darkness, often using a personal weakness or shadow quality as a way of entrapping us.[2] They are numinous and ambiguous, and they can be highly manipulative. Even if we turn to them for what we consider higher ends, these dark inner forces can tempt us and then use us for their own purposes.

Those who are seduced by them, or who consciously use them for their own power purposes, will find themselves in a demonic maze that is difficult to leave. There are no self-help guides for those who have gotten lost in the archetypal world. The story of Faust and Mephistopheles should be a warning, but we read it these days as a parable about the danger of ambition and greed; we do not realize that one really can sell one's soul for the dark powers of magic. As a culture we are caught by the glamour of worldly success and power. We have little understanding of the price these things exact from the soul. How will it be when we are given greater access to the real powers within life?

The darkness and deceptions of the inner world are real and they need to be acknowledged. Working with these energies requires constant vigilance and discrimination. Our consciousness is a balance to their seductive or devouring nature, to the pull into their dark depths. When we fall asleep we easily become the playthings of the gods. Remaining attentive, awake to the dangers, we can choose not to succumb to the shadows—we can choose the light. We can become a creative partner with these forces, and their power and understanding of the deep rhythms within life can bring new possibilities for a future civilization. Instead of imposing ourselves on life through force and violence as we have done for far too long, we can work together with it, in harmony with its flow.

THE WISDOM OF THE INNER

We can give the archetypes a voice in our world. We can learn to listen to their wisdom, their understanding of the primal patterns of creation. They have seen civilizations rise and fall, and they know the relationship of timelessness to time. They know the seasons of years and centuries; they know which part of the tree of life bears fruit and which part is barren. They can teach us when we can trust the serpent from the depths and when it is poisonous. They carry the real knowledge of our history, not the censored versions we have enshrined in our libraries. They can remind us of myths we have forgotten, knowledge we have lost. And they can show us the way into their world, and how to travel in the inner without getting lost. And then they can begin to show us their magic, ways of healing and transformation on an individual and collective level, ways of working with symbols and sound and other mediums whose inner secrets we have lost access to.

These powers can teach us how to flow with life's flow, so that our energies can be used creatively instead of being squandered in ineffectual attempts to defend ourselves against our fears or in resistance to changes we do not understand. They can teach us to protect ourselves against the real dangers we face, give us talismans and incantations to shield us from the forces of darkness and life's negative energies. They can help us to counter and undo the spell of materialism, to free humanity from this life-draining dream.

And they can teach us how to subvert some of the forces that today's corporations use in their drive to dominate. Why should we leave all the tricks of seduction and deception to those who would bend life to the agenda of their private greed and self-interest? Can we not put the ancient ways of cunning in service to life, to assist the whole of life at this moment of its awakening? When Christ advised his disciples, "Be ye therefore as wise as serpents," he was passing on a wisdom known to sages and mystics down through the ages.

Life always gives us what we need, if we know how to listen. The inner world is not a fantasy kingdom we enter only in our dreams, but a part of life. If we make a relationship with it, we will be forming a *coniunctio*, an alchemical union through which the sacred is reborn. And an important element of the sacred relationship to life born of this union will be the gift of the wisdom of the inner: the knowledge of how to use its almost limitless power to heal and transform, to free the world from a devouring darkness.

The darkness that grips our contemporary world also comes from the inner. It is a subversion of life's energies, an inner life force that has turned against itself and become destructive. It is the product of our hubris, our rejection of the sacred feminine and dismissal of the real power of the inner world in our drive to dominate and control life. Solving our outer problems will not loosen its grip: they are its surface symptoms, not its source. Only by turning back to the inner world and welcoming it back into life can we release the real forces that can dispel the darkness and allow life once again to flow and sustain the world. Only by making a conscious relationship with the archetypal world can we make our fragmented world whole again.

We are the doorway through which the gods can return to our world. Through our individual consciousness they can make a direct connection with the world of human consciousness. An individual cannot change the patterns and thought-forms of the collective; they are far too dense. But the archetypal world has the power to move collective consciousness, to infuse it with new, more beneficial thought-forms[3]—often with far-reaching collective consequences. We witnessed this dynamic at work in the collapse of the Berlin wall, when an archetype of freedom took hold in a whole nation of people and unexpectedly liberated it from the grip of a highly organized and effective repressive government. But the archetypal energies needed to bring about such changes in the collective can only work, paradoxically, through the individual— it is our individual conscious relationship to them that allows them to come into play in our world.

Our dismissal of the inner has caused it to suffer, and it has caused our world to suffer as well. Through our rejection we have imprisoned the primal energies of life in the depths of the archetypal world, and we have cut both inner and outer off from the dynamic energy of life that needs to flow through the connections between them if life is to flourish. Life is a single, living, dynamic wholeness that includes both outer and inner, surface and depths, and only together can we evolve, only together fulfill our shared destiny. Our consciousness *is* the connection between them: it is the key to life's future. Our conscious relationship with the inner world can reawaken it to the knowing of its divine purpose, and it can catalyze an alchemical transformation in the depths of the inner world; it can speed up changes there that normally unfold over millennia. And it can help us in the evolution of our outer world, in the way that humanity lives, in the way that it changes. Our consciousness gives a voice to the archetypes, which, as Jung says, "decide the fate of man." Through their expression in all its forms we can explore our destiny; we can come to understand humanity's role as guardians of the planet.

The book of life is written in the language of the inner as well as the outer world, and only when the worlds are working together can its meaning be revealed. From this *coniunctio* a new way of being can come into existence, a way of being that is based on life's oneness. It will confer on us a much greater responsibility, as we finally cease being the victims of life's primal powers and step into our co-creative role with life in the shaping of its future. But it will also bring the harmony and wisdom and new creativity that belong to life's next chapter.

7.

WORKING WITH DIFFERENT DIMENSIONS

The breath of the morning wind
will soon spread the fragrance of musk,
and the world will become young again.

Hâfez[1]

RECONNECTING THE WORLDS

In our dialogue with the awakening light of the world, we are being asked to bring the light of our consciousness to the archetypal world, to recognize and respect it and to relate consciously to its primal energies, in order to help midwife the symbols of the coming era. But there are other dimensions as well within our awakening world—it is a living being, made up of many different levels of reality. If we are to work with the world in its wholeness, we will need to bring our attention to these other levels as well. We will need to rediscover the esoteric knowledge of how the world works on all these different levels, as a living spiritual being. Through this knowledge we will come to know its different energies and regain access to its different levels of reality, rediscover how they function together, and how energy flows between them.

Our world contains within it centers of power, energy sources that belong to its functioning as a spiritual being. Some of these energy sources nourish the outer body of the world; in past eras these have been channeled in order to help the crops to grow, for example, or the rains to fall. Other energy sources belong primarily to the inner functioning of the world. These work with the ways its spiritual bodies interpenetrate and nourish each other. The world is sustained by the energies that belong to its inner bodies; it needs this nourishment in the same way that the individual needs to be nourished by the inner realm of the soul. The particular way these centers of power within the world work changes from era to era, as the energy sources are activated and their energy channeled according to the need of the time as the world evolves. How this works, and how energy flows from the inner to the outer, belong to the ancient esoteric knowledge of the world. Now as we move into this next stage of our evolution, a new facet of this knowledge is emerging that relates to the new responsibility that individual consciousness has been given in this unfolding—how we can direct our consciousness to work with life's different dimensions.

At the end of any era the old ways no longer work, no longer fulfill life's changing needs. This is part of the larger cycle of life. Old ways die out and new ones are born. But there is always a danger that the birth of the new ways will not be harmonious or beneficial. Just as the birth of a child is a dangerous passage for both mother and newborn, so is the birth of a civilization a perilous transition for the world. The present abyss between the inner and outer life is especially dangerous, as it has destroyed the normal patterns that keep life in balance and harmony. Humanity has even forgotten that the world has a soul. The energy needed to nourish the world cannot flow properly from inner to outer, cannot find the channels that meet the real needs of life. At such times it is easy for the forces of darkness to subvert the process of transformation and use any awakening energy to feed their own life-denying needs and desires. We see this at work now in our world, in the way the dynamics of globalization, which belong to the oneness of the future, are being manipulated by the self-serving forces of economic exploitation and greed. And the priests of our present religions seem unable to affect these forces; they have long lost access to the power or knowledge needed to bring the world back into balance. Instead, the energy that is being released as the world moves towards globalization, appears to be merely accelerating the pollution of the planet and the impoverishment of its soul. And we seem impotent to change this.

But within the world itself, in its inner centers of power, lie energies that can dissolve some of these negative patterns that are stifling us. And when we bring our consciousness to them, we can work together with them; we can help those energies to flow once again from the inner to the outer so that they can do their work. Our attention can be used to remove blocks that hinder the flow of energy, to direct energy where it is needed. We can also align their power with specific work that needs to be done in the outer world—to help free the energy of globalization that belongs to the future from the forces of greed and exploitation, for example, in the fields of global economics, trade, and even politics. It is no longer enough that this inner energy be used just to help the crops to grow; outer life and our needs have become vastly more complex. The spiritual transformation of the present time needs to include all levels of life, from growing and distributing enough food to feed the whole of humanity, to nourishing its collective soul. There is always enough energy, always enough resources; the work is how to distribute and balance the energy so that it goes where it is needed and contributes to the well-being of the whole.

If we are to heal the split between inner and outer and step into an awareness of oneness that is the paradigm of the future, we need to acknowledge the different levels on which life functions, and to recognize how they work together as part of an interrelated whole. We also need to recognize that we ourselves function at these different levels: that we exist not only in the familiar physical world of the senses, but also in the symbolic world of archetypal images, on the plane of the Self which is a world of pure love and pure consciousness, and beyond that on the planes of nonexistence, the void of the mystics. Human consciousness has the capacity to be awake in these different worlds, and it can move back and forth between them.[2] At this time of transition, we need to recognize our participation in all these different worlds, and to learn to work consciously with them.

One of the challenges of working with different dimensions is that they move at different speeds and follow different laws. The physical world is the most dense and slow-moving of the worlds and appears the most fixed. In the symbolic world images can shift and change, as we know from our dreams. Here we are not imprisoned by laws of gravity or the inertia that governs the material forms of the physical world. A shaman who works here is sometimes known as a shape-shifter; he can metamorphose from one form to another, become an eagle soaring in the sky, a fish, a wind. The plane of the Self is subject to even fewer constraints. It is not constricted by the laws of duality; it functions according to the ways of oneness in which everything is present at the same moment in the same space—the world in a grain of sand. This dimension moves so quickly it sometimes seems not to move at all; it is "the still center of the turning wheel."

Working with these different dimensions means being able to move freely from one set of laws to another, from one vibration or speed of consciousness to another. It means not getting caught in any fixed understanding of how things are. How things appear in the physical world may be quite different from how they are perceived in the symbolic dimension, and that appearance is even more different from the way they are perceived by the Self, which barely registers separation and multiplicity. And in the planes of nonbeing the appearances of this world do not even exist. This does not mean one abandons or rejects the laws of a particular world, however limited and even unreal they might appear from the point of view of other worlds. In order to function in our physical world one needs the awareness of multiplicity. One cannot go shopping in the supermarket with the sole consciousness that everything is one: how could one choose what to buy? Similarly if one brought the awareness of nonexistence, the knowing that nothing and no one really exists, into dealing with a speeding ticket, one would encounter unnecessary, even if nonexistent, problems. To work with the archetypal energies, too, one needs to recognize their existence and engage with the multiplicity of their forms and patterns. We are here to participate in the many worlds we inhabit; the key is not to get caught in any one of them but to be able to move freely between them, so that we do not limit how our consciousness can be used.

DIFFERENT FACULTIES OF PERCEPTION

The different levels of reality are accessed through different faculties of perception. We perceive the outer physical world through the five senses, which we then process with the mind and ego. The symbolic world is traditionally experienced and explored through the faculty of active or creative imagination.[3] The dimension of the Self is perceived through the single eye of the heart, the pure consciousness of the Self that belongs to our higher nature. The natural oneness of life is an expression of the Self, and it is the higher consciousness of the Self that most purely perceives it. But oneness can also be experienced through our instinctual nature, which is directly connected to life's wholeness and interconnectedness. Instinctual knowing is another faculty of perception; part of the tragedy of our culture is that we have lost our connection to it and thus lost access to this most natural and accessible way of experiencing the wholeness of life, which allows us to know life as an expression of divine oneness.

We all have these different faculties of perception within us, although the senses are obviously most accessible. We can, through practice, gain access to the other faculties as well. Developing active imagination is a simple practice of opening to the symbolic world in a state of receptive consciousness, (in the shamanic tradition one journeys into it) and welcoming its images into one's consciousness. In this state of inner awareness one can witness the formation of symbols and watch them change and transform; one can also learn to engage with the inner figures that appear, speak to them, have them respond about their nature and their needs. The pure consciousness of the Self is traditionally realized through spiritual practice, particularly meditation, which stills the continual chattering of the lower mind. Gradually one develops an awareness that is not based upon duality and separation but has the simplicity of direct perception. This is a state of knowing in which there is no separation between knowledge and knower. Through the eye of the heart everything is seen according to its true nature, both as uniquely individual and as one with all of creation. Instinctual consciousness is a natural way of knowing in which the individual is attuned to life, which can communicate directly without the barriers of developed consciousness. It may be difficult in our present culture to reclaim this way of knowing, however, since it often involves living in close communion with nature.

Working with the different dimensions means acknowledging these different modes of perception, developing an ability to work with them, and then being able to shift levels when required. Each has its own purpose in relation to the whole, and moving between them we can help them to work together. When the different worlds work together, the whole of life begins to flourish. When the symbolic and physical worlds are linked together, for example, outer life can be nourished by the numinosity of the soul, its sacred energy and meaning. Through this connection the archetypes can also be transformed and can work in new ways with the outer world. Energies within creation that have been long hidden can begin to reveal themselves and a quality of joy and magic return to life.

At the center of the archetypal world is the Self. Consciousness on the level of the Self is itself a bringing together of worlds, a vital contribution to life. When, even for an instant, one can hold the awareness of life's oneness of which one is a part— "The smallest grain of sand, myself and all else, part of the great magnificent chord echoing forever."[4]—one gives back to life an awareness of its single source, not as an idea but as a lived experience. To hear this chord, to know life's essential nature, nourishes life more than one is aware. For the individual and for life itself the awareness of the Self is a celebration of our divine nature in which everything is loved and known for its true self, and when that awareness is brought to the physical and symbolic worlds through our consciousness, all of life benefits.

Then beyond the Self there are the mystical states of nonbeing, in which the essential nonexistence of everything is realized. This also has an important purpose in the cycle of creation, an awareness of the primal emptiness that underlies the created worlds—though its very nonexistence means that nothing can be said!

Working with different worlds requires common sense and groundedness. In this work we stay grounded in the whole, which means not getting attached to one particular world or mode of perception, but remaining free to move between them. It is all too easy to get caught inside one world, identified with a single mode of perception. We know the attractions of the physical world and its web of desires, the pull of the senses or the mental appeal of the rational. The other worlds have seductions of their own kinds with which we may be less familiar. The gods of the archetypal world can draw us siren-like into their fascinating realm, tempting us with the chance to play some archetypal role—to be a hero, a goddess, a healer. Enticed into the labyrinth of the inner worlds, we are easily lost, our consciousness or sense of self devoured by the monsters of the depths. Our mental hospitals are home to many people who have never returned to the surface world of ordinary consciousness.

The dimension of the Self holds its own attractions. Who wants to return to a world of duality and shadows when one has been immersed in the clear light of oneness? Why accept the limitations of time and space when one knows the infinite eternal nature of one's real Self? For most people there is no choice; their experience of the Self is just a moment "in and out of time," an instant of pure presence, oneness, or unconditional love. Then they are back in their ego-self, sensing something wonderful has been given but also lost again.

But there are experiences of a deeper immersion in the Self. Traditionally these are given only to those who are mature enough to be able to return to the ego, to accept the constrictions of everyday life.[5] There can, however, be a demanding and confusing period of transition. Irina Tweedie describes the difficulties of reconciling the different levels of awareness after her teacher died, which caused her to go into retreat in the Himalayas for some months:

> I couldn't reconcile the torment of the heat, the mangy dogs roaming the streets, stone-throwing children, the sweat, the smells; for they were *That* too…. And the only thing to do was to run away into the solitude. It was here in the stillness of the mountains that it gradually crystallized itself—no, crystallized is not the right word—it "distilled" itself from a different dimension into the waking consciousness.[6]

Later the awareness of the Self remains amidst everyday consciousness, as a presence, a peace, or a quality of love. But one also has to acknowledge the divisions of this world. It requires strength of character to be able to live in different worlds, particularly to accept the limitations of a "lower" level of consciousness when one knows another reality.

THE SHADOWS OF DIFFERENT WORLDS

The different worlds can also evoke different shadow dynamics. Our shadow is the dark side of our ego-self and belongs to its world of duality. Our experiences in different worlds can affect the ego and its dark twin in different ways, and we need to be aware of these dynamics. We know the shadows of our physical, emotional, and mental world, the abuses of power, the deceits and cruelty we enact with ourselves and with others. We experience how addictions can creep in through weaknesses in our character, and we know the patterns of exploitation and greed that play on these addictions in our individual and collective life. We see the pain and suffering caused by our collective darkness, the divisions of rich and poor, powerful and weak. If we look, we can see how the moralities of good and bad, light and dark, which supposedly protect us from too much darkness, in reality create a shadow behind us as we walk through the world.

The archetypal world casts its own shadows. We can readily see the temptation it presents to use its energies or symbols for the power purposes of the ego, forgetting what one wants. But it also affects the ego in ways that may be less apparent. Part of the attraction of this inner world is its lack of definition, the sense that "one thing is never one thing." This fluidity allows us to explore and experience a magical and changing tapestry that is as rich as our imaginative self. Children inhabit this world with ease, and we can see it in their play: a cardboard box becomes a palace, the child inside it a princess. But adults are also drawn by the allure of this fantastic kingdom in which one can be a god or goddess, a magician or the Queen of the Night. This numinous world, where spells as well as magical swords and healing waters are real, can easily bewitch us; it can cause us to lose the groundedness of common sense, to lose interest in the relationships and responsibilities of everyday life. But what is the value of reclaiming our magical inner self if it makes us forget to pay our bills or help our own children with their homework?

In seducing us with its powers and its myriad possibilities, the archetypal world casts its shadow into our everyday life. Another, darker shadow from that world is the danger of inflation it poses to the ego, the danger of identifying with an archetype without the discrimination of consciousness. One actually believes that one is a hero, say, or a savior, in outer life. In that identification we forget our ordinariness. We might, like the figure in the fairy tale or myth who is turned to stone or ice, lose the warmth of human feeling. We could become imperious and demanding, the way a god or goddess, for example, demands rather than asks, assuming others must obey. Our personal shadow can also become inflated, even demonic, become obsessive or tyrannical. Identifying with an archetype often makes us arrogant, cold, and dismissive of ordinary values—courtesy and kindness are not a part of our heroic mission. You can see the darkness of an archetype at work when such simple human qualities are missing. And what is the point of a grand venture if we lose our humanity?

In the oneness of the Self there is no shadow, no split between light and dark. Everything exists according to its true nature and there is no judgmental self; there is just an observer, the one who witnesses. However, when we return into ordinary consciousness, the experience of the Self can carry a dark side. It can create a cold detachment, or a subtle feeling of superiority, a sense that one is now above the ordinary things of life. One may feel that one should not have to be involved in making money or engaging with other people's pettiness, their egos or their shadow sides. Or one may begin to take oneself or one's spiritual realizations too seriously—the ego may try to identify with the experience and become inflated, particularly if one lacks the capacity to laugh at oneself and the inconsistencies of life. One can even believe that one's experience of the Self is *the experience, the answer,* rather than just a momentary immersion in a changeless and yet an ever-changing vaster Reality. The true Self is a center of compassion, deep understanding, real freedom, and unconditional love, qualities that belong to true detachment. But its effect on the ego can cast a shadow, creating spiritual illusions or allowing undeveloped parts of one's character to dominate. It takes time to learn real discrimination. This is why the Sufis stress the importance of common sense and *adab*—courtesy, respect, and good behavior. Through *adab* we develop a character that can embody the highest principles of the Self and avoid becoming caught in negative patterns of behavior. Just as we need to look after our physical body, to exercise, eat good food, and avoid excess, we also need to develop a good character with qualities of humility and patience as well as strength and common sense that can contain the higher vibrations of the Self, in order to live the higher principles of our divine nature.

Working in different worlds requires a greater responsibility and awareness than we have been used to. Having access to the energies from the inner worlds gives our shadow more power, and also gives it new ways to deceive us. The archetypal world in particular can teach it new techniques of cunning and manipulation—the gods and goddesses have over millennia mastered the art of seducing, manipulating, and deceiving human beings. The different dimensions can affect our shadow in unexpected ways, and we need to be continually attentive, watching for shifts in outer or inner behavior that indicate that the ego or shadow has co-opted part of the experience for itself. We should always return to simple human values, like kindness, cooperation, generosity, that show our respect for the life of which we are a part, which we know as both ordinary and divine.

ALCHEMICAL DIALOGUE WITH LIFE

One of the changes of this time of transition is that one no longer needs to be an adept to work in the inner worlds. One does not need to be a shaman or alchemist to work with life's symbols. Many people use active imagination in dreamwork, painting, dance, or other mediums to access and work with the images of the archetypal world. Similarly one does not need to be fully awakened to participate in the work of the Self. Most spiritual practitioners have had a moment of pure presence or inner peace that has given them access to this dimension. We can participate in this work as long as we know that these worlds are within us and within life and we are open and willing to engage. This is part of the freedom of this time: nothing is separate and no one is excluded. We only exclude ourselves.

We also need to have the humility and receptivity to be attentive to what life needs of us. In life's wholeness nothing is more or less important—each is part of an organic self-sustaining whole. Some people are more in harmony with the archetypal world and can be receptive to its transforming symbols. Others are by nature attracted to the simplicity and ordinariness of the Self and its quality of presence. Each world makes different demands, and there are different ways of being attuned to its needs, different ways to participate in its energy. Life draws our attention to where we are needed, where we can participate most creatively. We limit ourselves and our usefulness when we become fixed in a particular mode of thought or attitude that stops us from being receptive, that veils us from what life is communicating. If we are as open as possible, life will communicate with us and a creative dialogue can then ensue—a dialogue between the light of the world and our individual light. This dialogue is in itself an alchemical interaction and it carries a quality of joy that belongs to life awakening to what it really is.

As we shift between levels of consciousness, we will begin to discover that life can expand in unexpected ways. Much of the feeling of constriction that we experience in our life is caused by the ways we limit ourselves, imprison ourselves in conditioning and a particular mode of perception. Life is alive on many different levels, and when we open to the ways these levels can interact with each other and with us, we will find ourselves present in a very different world—one that is more dynamic and flexible than we now believe possible. Just as the shaman's capacity to shift from one shape to another frees him from the limitations of his outer human form, we will find that the way the worlds interpenetrate within us and within life frees us from many of our apparent limitations. Life and consciousness are much less fixed, much more fluid and dynamic, than we presently experience.

The alchemical dialogue between our individual consciousness and life is itself a dynamic and constantly changing process. Once we allow life to communicate with us directly, rather than through the veils of our conditioning, we can become present in life's constantly changing interaction with itself. Life is continually experimenting, trying new ways to survive and evolve, new ways to reveal His oneness. And often there is a quality of fun in this dance of revelation as the different worlds flow together, communicating with each other. Our rational conditioning has divorced our consciousness from this dynamic interchange, but once we leave behind these fixed thought-patterns, life can invite us back into its intoxicating exploration of what it means to be alive.

One has just to step outside on a spring morning, or dig into a compost heap, to see life in its abundance.

Every cloud is unique, and even in the cities we can hear the songs of so many birds. We blinker ourselves against any distraction from our defined material goals, but life is constantly distracting itself, with smells, sounds, dreams, storms, turning its attention in myriad directions at once. Every moment is an unimaginable abundance, offering an infinite possibility of experiences. And at this time of transition, every moment is also teeming with the chaos of creation, as life recreates itself yet again, dissolving old forms and giving birth to new ways of being. And we are a central part of this orgasmic revelation: our consciousness can be present at the moment of conception when forms are born and life tries once again to point to His truth.

As the different levels interpenetrate within our consciousness, we will free not just ourselves from the prison of our fixed ways of seeing; we will also free life from many of the restrictions it has suffered from our rational constrictions. As our consciousness expands, life can also expand and use energies that our fixed consciousness has blocked. Human consciousness holds the key to many of the secrets of creation—this is an aspect of our role as guardians of the planet. Without our participation, many of life's hidden energies remain dormant, locked in the inner planes. The knowledge that shamans and priestesses used to unlock these energies for their people and their land we need to rediscover now. We have to awake to what it really means to be alive on different levels of consciousness, and to the responsibility this gives us. The inner worlds need our attention in order to release the energies without which life will stagnate or even die. This is why life will draw our attention to where it is needed.

Once we realize that we are each a part of life, we can understand and trust that life knows our real potential and how to engage us. We are a part of life's cellular structure, and just as our body knows the cells that make it up and their individual purpose in relation to its functioning as a whole, so does life know each of us. It knows where our unique abilities are needed, where our consciousness can participate most creatively. We just need to recognize that we are a part of this creative experience and to be receptive to life as it speaks to us, as it draws our attention back to itself. And it is through the dialogue of light with light, the light of our consciousness with the light within life itself, that the intelligence within life can most directly communicate with our intelligence, can help us to fully participate in this mystery that is happening within and around us.

THE END OF EXILE

Once the different levels of creation relate together in our consciousness, a change will take place. As our patterns of separation fall away, we will find ourselves present in a very different world, one more fully alive and unexpected. Certain constraints that we have imposed upon life will fall away and we will have access to energies within life that have been dormant—doors within life and within our consciousness that have been closed will open. And this is just the beginning. The next step will be to consciously engage with this expanded circle of life, with its interpenetrating levels of reality that are in continual communication with each other, as in the image of the angels ascending and descending the ladder between heaven and earth, from Jacob's dream in the book of Genesis.[7]

In Jacob's dream in the Genesis story, God, standing above the top of the ladder, blesses him and his descendants, gives him the land on which he is lying, and says, "Behold, I am with thee." This affirmation of divine presence in this world is a blessing we have forgotten, a blessing that contains all the levels of creation, from heaven to earth, in constant relationship: the angels ascending and descending. Waking from his dream, Jacob says, "Surely the Lord is in this place: and I knew it not."[8] And so for us: now we know it not; now we live as exiles from God in this world. But as we engage consciously with the invisible and visible worlds as they relate together, we can replace this sense of exile with a knowing of divine presence.

As the different worlds commune together, something can be given from the highest directly into our world, given without the medium of priests or ceremonies. The one to One relationship of the individual and the divine can be re-established. There was a time when humanity could hear the voice of God in the garden of life, before Adam and Eve hid themselves from His presence. When our natural relationship with the divine is re-established, our exile can finally end, and we will once again be able to hear Him in His world—hear His voice in all of the sounds of creation as well as in the silence, see His signs as they are around us and within us. And this will be nothing esoteric but simply a part of life.

Then a certain sorrow will be lifted from humanity, a certain pain will be released. This world will always contain suffering; it is part of the nature of physical life. But a sorrow born of exile from our Creator will be gone, as we will come to know more consciously that we are a part of Him, part of the outpouring of His love. Then many of the toys that we use to distract ourselves from this sorrow will lose their attraction, many of the addictions that cover this pain will no longer be necessary. Something simple can return, a simple respect for ourselves and each other, a simple recognition of the divine within life, a simpler way of living. This may take time, as it will take a while for us to let go of our patterns of protection and all our distracting toys, which now seem so central to our existence. But life is more forgiving than we know, and we do not need to carry the clothes of winter too far into spring.

8.

THE WATERS OF LIFE

*We live by mystery
and not by explanations.*

Cecil Collins

A NEW SPRING IS BORN

Each age begins with an impulse of new energy. This energy carries the divine intentions of the new era; it contains the qualities, like love, knowledge, beauty, or compassion, that belong to those divine intentions. It flows into the world from the beyond as a pure energy, helping humanity to evolve.

Coming into humanity, it develops the structures it needs to support it. Initially, these structures allow the energy to flow freely, according to its divine intentions, infusing life with its vision and its qualities. But over the centuries these structures tend to become corrupted, appropriated by baser human purposes. The energy that created them can no longer flow freely, and slowly it loses its divine imprint, the inner intention of the age. The era of Christianity, for example, began with a vision of divine love and self-sacrifice, which after Christ's crucifixion was carried by the twelve apostles. But over time the structure that had initially supported that vision was taken over by the hierarchies of the church, which turned its energy to the purposes of its own power—its endless power struggles, the Crusades, the Inquisition. Our scientific age, as another example, was born from a vision of order, clarity, knowledge, and progress. But what began as an understanding of the forces governing our physical world, that freed humanity from the endless round of chaotic nature and ushered in a new era of consciousness and progress, soon became an instrument of soul-denying control and manipulation. Science and its primary tool, rational thought, expunged the divine from within life and turned the physical world into dead matter, a mere mechanism. We now live in the soulless, machine-driven culture that has resulted.

This is the way of our world: slowly humanity corrupts what it is given. The energy gets polluted and no longer flows freely. Its initial divine quality gets lost, and humanity's lower nature, the ego's patterns of greed and control, take over. And then the energy withdraws. This cycle is simply described in Carl Jung's favorite story: One day the water of life decided it wanted to spring up and be a source of new life for all people. When it did, the people began to gather to share in its bounty. Before long, those who had discovered its gifts felt the need to protect it. They put a fence around it and a guard to watch over it. Someone else put a lock on the gate. Soon others began to ration it and to decide who could drink from it and who could not. Then someone wanted to sell it and make money off its sweet, refreshing taste. As a result, the water, which was life, became a source of division and anger for those who had found it. This disturbed the water of life greatly, and the water decided it would cease flowing there and find another place to bubble forth, which is just what it did. And this has been going on ever since throughout all of history.

Each time the water of life moves to a new place, bubbling forth on a distant hillside, at first no one notices. Water still flows from the old spring for a time, and people do not notice that it has become just ordinary water that lacks the power of the water of life. It is still bottled and sold by those businesses and organizations that had grown up around the spring. Today the old water has been so well marketed that everyone still believes it is the water of life—that the meaning of life still lies in the pursuit of material well-being in which we have invested so much of our attention, our energy, and resources. Those who sell it have much to gain from that collective conviction, and they have become very clever at manipulating the dreams and fantasies of the collective so that no one will recognize it for the illusion it is.

But because this water no longer carries the real energy of life, everything around it will gradually die. This is a natural cycle, and one could decide not to interfere with it. One could just wait for it to play out, for the energy to be withdrawn from the present civilization and appear in a new way in a new place. This is how it has always happened through humanity's long evolution, and we too could just follow the deeper rhythms of life, withdraw our energy from the old ways, discover the new spring and take our attention there. But this cycle could take many generations to complete itself, and the water that is being marketed and sold has become so toxic that it now poses a danger to the whole planet.

In the previous chapters I have suggested that although this transition is a natural process that belongs to changes taking place in the very depths of creation, in the light at the core of the world, there is also a way to work with it consciously. Through our conscious participation we can alchemically speed up a process that might otherwise take centuries and cause untold further damage to the earth and its inhabitants. We can help the old ways to die and the new waters to flow where they are needed to heal and transform the land that is now being made into a wasteland; we can help create the images and forms of the new era that will help restore our world.

WE ARE THE NEW ENERGY

When the water of life moves to a new place, it might take centuries before it is discovered, before a new civilization can grow up around it and the new structures and ways develop that will make its life-giving properties available to humanity. The period between the withdrawal of the healing water from the old hillside and its reemergence as a life-giving source in its new location is often a dark age for humanity, a time in which there is little light to help human beings to live. One thinks of the dark ages that followed the decline of the Roman Empire in Europe, when the light of civilization seemed lost, when the constant warfare and brutality of local lords dominated the land. What has happened in the last decades in Tibet is a more recent example, with monks and nuns tortured, sacred texts and temples destroyed, and the light and wisdom of a vibrant spiritual culture banished.

If we are to avoid centuries of global desolation, we need to recognize the nature of the present time of transition. We need to discover the new source of life, and to help its energies to flow into humanity. Some will be drawn to work with the age that is awakening. They will be given the knowledge needed to do this work with life's primal energies and its archetypal patterns as they rearrange and reconstellate themselves, and with the images that will emerge from them which will help determine the shape of the coming age. Other souls are here to help the old world to die, to close down some of the energy structures that belong to the previous age and to help other structures that can be beneficial to make the transition into the new age. They will be given access to ways of using the powers of creation to dissolve some of the structures that are life-denying, and to transform others so that they can accommodate the new waters of life; they will also be given the knowledge to discriminate between what can be saved and what needs to die.

If we look around us we can see the depletion of our natural world, the corruption and incompetence of our governments, the greed of our corporations, the worsening condition of the poor and the indifference of those who live in comfort—we see the civilization that is dying. And if we look more closely we will see that *in the midst* of this decay the new water is also flowing. It is not on some distant hillside, some remote place. It is here, in the very midst of our lives, that the organic wholeness of life is reconstellating. The new age will be born not through a savior or an elite group of disciples, but through everyman, in a global awakening that is happening everywhere across the world. This awakening is already visible, in the many new ways that people are coming together. The healing waters of life are here, all around us, in these new patterns of relationship: in the fast-evolving network of global communication, in the coming together of individuals and small groups into new kinds of networks, in connections and relationships across all kind of boundaries that were never possible before—in the myriad new ways now emerging of relating to one another and to life.

We are the energy of life flowing from the Source. We are the place where the worlds meet, the place where life is re-forming itself. This is so simple it is easy to overlook. We are conditioned to look to the horizons, to search for grand schemes and well-thought-out solutions, and so we miss what is already happening in the midst of our daily lives. With the Internet and all the proliferating forms of global communication, individual human beings are communicating and relating in ways that would have been unimaginable only a few decades ago. We all use these tools of communication without being aware of what is happening: that through them life is reconstellating itself, new patterns of relationship are coming into being, and it is here that the new waters of life are beginning to flow. The energy of life is flowing through us, through these connections and networks that are being formed. We think of them as tools, ways of facilitating communication or commerce. We do not realize that what matters are the networks themselves, these developing patterns of interconnection and relationship.

If we look closely, we can see that no one is in charge of these patterns. They are continually forming, changing, re-forming, too free and fast-moving to be controlled or manipulated by any person or organization. They are alive in a completely new way: a life force in themselves. And they carry the light, the consciousness, of individuals. They are the light of individual consciousness, continually moving, changing, creating different patterns, communicating in new ways, in a dialogue of light with light, individual with individual. And this dialogue of light is going on around us, communicating through a vast web of interconnections all over the world, and we do not realize its significance.

Some places in the world seem to have more access to this global communication than others, to be more connected, their inhabitants less isolated. But there are few places that are out of touch. The spread of Internet cafés, even in apparently remote locations, reflects a worldwide hunger for global connectedness. We are all part of one humanity, and it is in this network of communication, in the simple connection of individual to individual through a spreading global web of connections, that the healing waters of life are springing up. Everyone participates in this connectedness. We have just not yet learned how to work with it, how to help the light that is coming alive again in these connections to redeem what has been desecrated, how to help it to heal our planet and our souls.

We are still focused on the old paradigm of treating problems in isolation, as if they existed separate from the whole web of conditions around them. But the problem *is* the isolation we have imposed on ourselves and our world, *is* our myth of separation. Only when we abandon this paradigm and step into an awareness of life's interconnected oneness can the energy of life teach us how to work with it, reconnect our individual consciousness with its primal energy and enable a real alchemy of transformation to take place. This has always been the way the energy of life has regenerated itself, working with the divine consciousness that is present in the planet. In previous ages, the divine consciousness was often held by a spiritual teacher and his disciples, like Christ and the apostles, and they were the first to work with the new energy of that era. They were saviors and transformers, pouring a new wine into new bottles to nourish humanity. But now humanity, individually and as a whole, is its own savior. We have to accept our responsibility for this. We all carry the light of divine consciousness, and we need to give this light back to the world. Then the world can come alive again: the waters of life will flow quickly where they are needed, and we can avoid centuries of darkness.

BEING PRESENT IN A MYSTERY

Once again we have to learn how to work with the divine, for without the spark of divine consciousness the world cannot alchemically transform. But this spark does not follow the laws of reason, the logic of our minds. It follows its own ways, which are the ways of the divine and the hidden ways of creation.

When the alchemists were working in their retorts and crucibles, they were often amazed at the results, at the strange and unexpected phenomena they observed as different chemicals combined. The same is true of the inner alchemical processes. Reason would not predict the phenomenon of *enantidromia*, for example, in which something turns into its opposite, as when the inner descent into hell becomes an ascent to the light—when, to quote Heraclitus, "the way up and the way down are one and the same."[1] The paradoxical nature of the inner world combined with the alchemical spark of divine light can produce strange and unexpected happenings and synchronicities. Do we dare to recognize that what happens within the individual could also happen within the larger body of the world? That the world does not need to follow the laws of science, but could have an alchemical dimension? Are we prepared for the unexpected, for the world to respond according to ancient inner laws of transformation that are quite different from our scientific myths?

When the light of the individual meets the sacred substance of life, something mysterious takes place—a strange magic is born. There is a magic inherent in matter of which we know little. There are secret forces within creation that are as strange to our conscious self as the creatures that swim in the dark depths of the ocean. Seeing life through the prism of our defined self, we allow ourselves our little insecurities and anxieties but do not dare to acknowledge the vaster unknown around us. Occasionally we might get caught up in unexplained passions or turbulent events; we might catch a glimpse of some miraculous happening; but mostly we pass our life close to the shore. We might sense there are deeper waters, whirlpools, strange currents, but we tend to dismiss them or busy ourselves with our daily activities. We have lost the respect for mystery possessed by our more primitive ancestors, who lived in relationship to the unknown, who were always aware of the darkness beyond the flickering light of their campfires.

We do not fully recognize that an era is ending, and that we are all entering the unknown. The future will not be shaped solely by the familiar forces we believe to be governing our present world. Other forces are constellating now that we do not yet know or understand, and that we cannot manipulate to our own ends. Can we acknowledge that we live in a world we cannot control, that is vaster and stranger than our present culture and conditioning allow for? Are we prepared to be present in such a world, one that is alive and full of magic and serving purposes beyond our own private concerns and desires? Are we willing to be a part of its awakening?

We are the crucible for the transformation of the whole: a network of those who have glimpsed beyond the censored consciousness of our present civilization into a future of other possibilities—a network organically created by life itself, linking together individuals and small groups who are not caught in life-denying images but are alive to the real potential of life. We are also the bridge between the inner and outer worlds, and the light of our divine consciousness is the spark that crosses this bridge and catalyzes the transformation of the whole. As a microcosm of the whole, we contain within us all these dimensions and possibilities, which belong to the real work of co-creating the world. This is a work of alchemy, and it is the nature of the alchemical process to produce the unexpected and the miraculous.

Through us the waters of life can come alive in a new way and bring their healing and revitalizing energy where it is needed, to places in the inner and outer world that belong to life's initial reawakening. The colors of this dawn are just becoming visible; the first birds can be heard if one listens closely. It is said that the darkest hour is just before dawn, when it seems the darkness will never end, and maybe this is our present moment. But the alchemists knew what nature knows, that this is the moment of change. And life sends its messengers into the darkness to remind us, to point us towards the dawn. The messenger always comes as a song of hope, a note of remembrance, an inner call to prayer. We just need to be present and receptive so that we can hear it and respond to the call. It is difficult for us to realize how much is being given, and how much has been prepared for this dawn. And yet it is all around us—not hidden, but just barely visible within our present patterns of consciousness.

As well as being receptive, we can bring our spiritual consciousness into life, into the flow of creation. What does this mean? It means to hold an awareness of the divine nature of life and the whole of which we are a part. There is a simple spiritual practice in which one recognizes the divine in another person, and we can take this practice into all of life: see His face wheresoever we turn. Wherever we look, whatever we touch, whatever we hear, we can be awake to the possibility of divine presence. We can learn once again to be present in His world, in His divine oneness that is all around us, in every breath we breathe.

Through this simple awareness we offer the spark of our divine consciousness back to life, where it works as an alchemical catalyst, the *Spirit Mercurius*, the messenger of the gods. We are the spark of the world, and alchemy is always transformation. It does not bring perfection, because it belongs to life. We do not know what will happen, how the future will unfold, because this is the light of the divine alive within life, the *lumen naturae* that carries the secrets of creation. But we can be a part of this unfolding, awake to the unexpected, bringing our wonder to what will be born. We can have faith in the ancient wisdom of creation, the knowing of the soul of the world. And for a moment we can step outside of the confines of our present conditioned consciousness, the buying and selling we call life, and be present in the real waters of life, the real mystery of the divine coming into form.

These chapters do not attempt to define the future, but to open a door that is normally kept closed, a door that leads to a creative participation in life *as it is*, with the living substance of creation and the forces that underlie our existence. They suggest that an alchemy can take place that can change our image of existence, our dream of life, and, more deeply, could change the very patterns of creation, the riverbeds through which life flows; and that we have a role to play in that process. But in order to take part in this experiment in consciousness, we have to be prepared to be alive, to live our own divine spark, without knowing into what world we will be born. We make a commitment to life as a whole, in all its mysterious strangeness and all its ordinariness. We do not know what will happen. We just know that there is a deep need for us to participate, to give ourselves, and to accept that life possesses wisdom and knowledge far beyond our present consciousness.

We are each being given the opportunity to be present at this moment in time, this catalytic moment of creation. Life is calling to us and it is for each of us to hear and respond to this call in our own way. And this is all part of the most strange and wonderful love affair of life, our life and the life of the world.

NOTES

1. WORKING WITH LIGHT

1. Quoted by Sarrâj, *Knowledge of God in Classical Sufism*, p. 90.
2. The poet William Wordsworth describes this sad transition:
   > Heaven lies about us in our infancy!
   > Shades of the prison-house begin to close
   > Upon the growing Boy
   > But He beholds the light and whence it flows.
   > He sees it in his joy; ...
   > At length the Man perceives it die away,
   > And fade into the light of common day.

   "Intimations of Immortality from Recollections of Early Childhood,"
   ll. 66-76. *Wordsworth Poetical Works*.
3. In the words of al-Jîlânî:
   > "It is not the stars that guide us but the divine light.... If only
   > the lamp of divine secrets be kindled in your inner self the
   > rest will come, either all at once or little by little.... The dark
   > skies of unconsciousness will be lit by the divine presence and
   > the peace and beauty of the full moon, which will rise from
   > the horizon shedding *light upon light*, ever rising in the sky,
   > passing through its appointed stages... until it shines in glory in
   > the center of the sky, dispersing the darkness of heedlessness....
   > Your night of unconsciousness will then see the brightness of
   > the day.... Then you will see from the horizon of Divine Reason
   > the sun of inner knowledge rising. It is your private sun for
   > you are the one *whom Allâh guides*.... Finally, the knot will
   > be untied... and the veils will lift and the shells will shatter,
   > revealing the fine beneath the coarse; the truth will uncover
   > her face.
   >
   > All this will begin when the mirror of your heart is
   > cleansed. The light of Divine secrets will fall upon it if you
   > are willing and ask for Him, from Him, with Him."

   'Abd al-Qâdir al-Jîlânî, *The Secret of Secrets*, trans. Shaykh Tosun
   Bayrak al-Jerrahi al-Halveti, pp. xlvii-xlviii.

2. THE LIGHT OF THE WORLD

1. St. Mark 8:36.
2. St. Matthew 5:14.

3. Najm al-Dîn Kubrâ, quoted by Henry Corbin, *Man of Light in Iranian Sufism*, p. 73.
4. Ibid.
5. Saint Teresa of Avila delineates a similar process in her stages of prayer. She uses the image of a gardener watering his garden to describe these stages. At the beginning the gardener must make every effort to lift the water from the well, but slowly the effort of the gardener becomes less and less, until in the final stage there is no longer a gardener, only the Lord Himself soaking the garden in abundant rain.
6. Rûmî, trans. Coleman Barks, *One-Handed Basket Weaving*, p. 14.
7. Hadîth.
8. Robert Wolff, *Original Wisdom*, pp. 174-175.
9. "Among School Children," *Collected Poems of W. B. Yeats*.

3. CONSCIOUSNESS AND CHANGE

1. Brother Lawrence (d. 1691) was a Carmelite lay brother, author of *The Practice of the Presence of God: The Best Rule of Holy Life*.
2. For example, there is a tradition that there is a spiritual center in Washington, DC situated under the Cathedral, and that the energy from this center belongs to the work of the capital.

4. IMAGES OF LIFE

1. "Byzantium," *Collected Poems of W. B. Yeats*, p. 281.
2. William Wordsworth, "Lines Composed a Few Miles Above Tintern Abbey," *Wordsworth Poetical Works*.
3. C. G. Jung, *Psychological Reflections*, p. 39.
4. Psalms 36:9.

5. CHANGING THE DREAM

1. Ode: 'We are the Music Makers.'
2. "An Offer They Can't Refuse," *The Sun*, September 2005, Issue 357, p. 11.
3. In recent years there has been a resurgence of interest in the West in shamanism, but practising shamans do not play the central role in the life of our Western culture that is needed to guide and transform a whole civilization.

4. Before the 2005 tsunami that caused so much loss of life, the nomadic Moken sailors who live among the islands in the Andaman Sea, off Myanmar (Burma), recognized the signs of the coming disaster in the dolphins and other fish suddenly swimming to deeper water. So they too took their boats further from the shore and rode out the waves, unlike the Burmese fishermen who were not attentive to the signs of nature but stayed close to shore where they perished as their boats were wrecked by the tsunami. The Moken said of the Burmese fishermen, "They were collecting squid, they were not looking at anything. They saw nothing, they looked at nothing. They don't know how to look."

5. "And he showed me a pure river of the water of life, clear as crystal, proceeding out of the throne of God and the Lamb." The Revelation of St. John the Divine 22:1.

6. And yet Christ being born in a stable should have prepared us for a new age to be born within the ordinary.

7. "The images of the unconscious place a great responsibility upon a man. Failure to understand them, or a shirking of ethical responsibility, deprives him of his wholeness and imposes a painful fragmentation upon his life." *Memories, Dreams, Reflections*, p. 218.

8. Perseus cuts off the snake-filled head of Medusa by only looking at her in his shield, which symbolizes the reflective stance of consciousness.

6. THE ALCHEMY OF THE ARCHETYPAL WORLD

1. See Vaughan-Lee, *Working with Oneness*, ch. 8, "Imagination" (pp. 111-124), for a description of the traditional use of the imagination in exploring the archetypal world.

2. Shakespeare's Othello shows how "the green-eyed monster jealousy" can destroy a brave and honorable man through a simple weakness in his character.

3. Of course the reverse is also true, as at a time of war when the warrior god evokes violent and destructive thought-forms.

7. WORKING WITH DIFFERENT DIMENSIONS

1. Hâfez, "The Song of Spring," *Dance of Life*, p. 12, adaptation.

2. There are also other worlds to which we have less direct access, like the world of the angels and the worlds of nature spirits and of other, darker entities, which are hidden from most people, though there are those who can see and communicate with them.

3. See Vaughan-Lee, *Working with Oneness*, pp. 112-114, for a description of active imagination's roots in alchemy and Sufism.
4. Irina Tweedie, *Daughter of Fire*, p. 813.
5. In some rare instances the individual who is taken into the world of the Self is unable or unwilling to return to ego-consciousness, as Suzanne Segal describes in her book *Collision with the Infinite*.
6. *Daughter of Fire*, p. 813.
7. Genesis 28:12-13.
8. Genesis 28:16.

8. THE WATERS OF LIFE

1. This is often experienced in a "creative illness."

BIBLIOGRAPHY

The Bible, Authorized Version. London: 1611.

Brother Lawrence. *The Practice of the Presence of God: The Best Rule of a Holy Life*. London: Samuel Baxter & Sons.

Corbin, Henry. *The Man of Light in Iranian Sufism*. London: Shambhala, 1978.

Hafez. *Dance of Life*, Trans. Michael Boylan and Wilberforce Clarke. Washington, DC: Mage Publishers, 1988.

Jami. *This Heavenly Wine: Renditions from the Divan-e Jami*. Renditions by Vraje Abramian. Prescott, AZ: Holm Press, 2006.

Jung, C. G. *Collected Works*. London: Routledge & Kegan Paul.

—. *Memories, Dreams, Reflections*. London: Flamingo, 1983.

—. *Psychological Reflections*. Ed. Jolande Jacobi. London: Routledge & Kegan Paul, 1953.

Perkins, John. "An Offer They Can't Refuse." *The Sun*, September 2005, Issue 357.

Renard, John. *Knowledge of God in Classical Sufism*. Mahwah, NJ: Paulist Press, 2004.

Rumi. *One-Handed Basket Weaving*. Trans. Coleman Barks. Athens, GA: Maypop Books, 1991.

Segal, Suzanne. *Collision with the Infinite*. San Diego, CA: Blue Dove Press, 1996.

Tagore, Rabindranath. *Collected Poems and Plays of Rabindranath Tagore*. London: Macmillan, 1936.

Teresa of Avila. *Interior Castle*. New York: Doubleday, 1989.

Tweedie, Irina. *Daughter of Fire: A Diary of a Spiritual Training with a Sufi Master*. Inverness, CA: Golden Sufi Center, 1986.

Vaughan-Lee, Llewellyn. *Working with Oneness*. Inverness, CA: The Golden Sufi Center, 2002.

Wolff, Robert. *Original Wisdom*. Rochester, VT: Inner Traditions, 2001.

Wordsworth, William. *Wordsworth Poetical Works*. Ed. Thomas Hutchinson. Oxford: Oxford University Press, 1969.

Yeats, W. B. *Collected Poems of W. B. Yeats*. London: Macmillan, 1933.

INDEX

ACKNOWLEDGMENTS

For permission to use copyrighted material, the author gratefully wishes to acknowledge: Paulist Press, Inc. for permission to use excerpts from *Knowledge of God in Classical Sufism*, translated and introduced by John Renard, preface by Ahmet T. Karamstafa, Copyright © 2004 by John Renard. Paulist Press, Inc., New York/Mahwah, NJ, www.paulistpress.com; Inner Traditions for permission to quote from *Original Wisdom: Stories of an Ancient Way of Knowing* by Robert Wolff, Inner Traditions, Rochester, VT, 05767, Copyright © 2001 by Robert Wolff, www.innertraditions.com; Hohm Press for permission to quote from *This Heavenly Wine: Renditions from the Divan-e Jami* by Vraje Abramian, www.hohmpress.com, Copyright © 2006 Vraje Abramian; Pat MacEnulty for excerpt from interview with John Perkins, "An Offer They Can't Refuse," originally printed in *The Sun*, Issue 357, September 2005, www.thesunmagazine.org, www.patmacenulty.com, Copyright © 2005 Pat MacEnulty; and The Islamic Texts Society for excerpt from *Secret of Secrets* by Abd al-Qâdir al-Jîlânî, Copyright © 1992 Islamic Texts Society.

ABOUT *the* AUTHOR

LLEWELLYN VAUGHAN-LEE, Ph.D., is a Sufi teacher in the Naqshbandiyya-Mujaddidiyya Sufi Order. Born in London in 1953, he has followed the Naqshbandi Sufi path since he was nineteen. In 1991 he became the successor of Irina Tweedie, author of *Daughter of Fire: A Diary of a Spiritual Training with a Sufi Master*. He then moved to Northern California and founded The Golden Sufi Center (www.goldensufi.org).

Author of several books, he has specialized in the area of dreamwork, integrating the ancient Sufi approach to dreams with the insights of Jungian Psychology. Since 2000 his writing and teaching has been on spiritual responsibility in our present time of transition, and an awakening global consciousness of oneness (www.workingwithoneness.org). More recently the focus of his work has been in the emerging field of spiritual ecology (www.spiritualecology.org). He has been interviewed by Oprah Winfrey on Super Soul Sunday, and featured on the Global Spirit Series shown on PBS.

ABOUT *the* PUBLISHER

THE GOLDEN SUFI CENTER is a California Religious Non-Profit Corporation dedicated to making the teachings of the Naqshbandi Sufi path available to all seekers. For further information about the activities and publications, please contact:

THE GOLDEN SUFI CENTER
P.O. Box 456 · Point Reyes Station · CA · 94956-0456
tel: 415-663-0100 · *fax:* 415-663-0103
info@goldensufi.org · www.goldensufi.org

*A complete list of publications
is available at www.goldensufi.org*

ABOUT WORKING *with* ONENESS

www.workingwithoneness.org

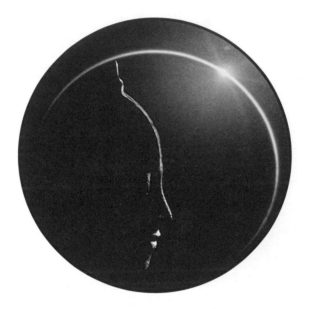

This site offers a body of teachings on the spiritual dimension of oneness. It is dedicated to connecting with spiritual groups of all types who are working towards the emerging consciousness of oneness. Consciousness of oneness is an awareness of the unity and interconnectedness of all of life. This is central to our human and planetary survival and evolution.

At the present time there is a greater need for those of us drawn to this work of oneness to connect with each other. We hope this website will be a valuable resource for you in facilitating this connection.

Please visit our website, www.workingwithoneness.org
for resources and information on upcoming
events and publications, or contact us at
info@workingwithoneness.org.